La Fontaine

Twayne's World Authors Series
French Literature

David O'Connell, Editor
University of Illinois at Chicago

TWAS 788

JEAN de LA FONTAINE
Né a Château Thierry   Mort a Paris
1621   1695

LA FONTAINE
(1621–1695)
Portrait by Auguste Sandoz
after a painting by Hyacinthe Rigaud.
Engraved by F. Delannoy in Album,
Oeuvres de La Fontaine (*Paris Hachette, 1897*).

La Fontaine

By Marie-Odile Sweetser

University of Illinois at Chicago

Twayne Publishers
A Division of G. K. Hall & Co. • *Boston*

La Fontaine

Marie-Odile Sweetser

Copyright © 1987 by G.K. Hall & Co.
All Rights Reserved
Published by Twayne Publishers
A Division of G.K. Hall & Co.
70 Lincoln Street, Boston, Massachusetts 02111

Copyediting supervised by Lewis DeSimone
Book production by Marne B. Sultz
Book design by Barbara Anderson
Typeset in 11 pt. Garamond
by Modern Graphics, Inc., Weymouth, Massachusetts

Printed on permanent/durable acid-free paper
and bound in the United States of America

Library of Congress Cataloging in Publication Data

Sweetser, Marie Odile.
    La Fontaine.

    (Twayne's world authors series; TWAS 788. French literature)
    Bibliography: p. 149
    Includes index.
    1. La Fontaine, Jean de, 1621–1695—Criticism and
interpretation.   2. Fables, French—History and
criticism.   I. Title.   II. Series.
PQ1812.S84   1987   841'.4   86–18295
ISBN 0–8057–6639–1

For my daughter, Caroline, who has a way with words and
asked to have a book dedicated to her
With great affection

Contents

About the Author

Born and raised in France, Marie-Odile Sweetser became acquainted with La Fontaine's *Fables* at an early age. She attended the University of Nancy where she received a licence ès-lettres and diplôme d'études supérieures. She came to the United States with a scholarship from Bryn Mawr College where she received her M.A. After a two year stint at McGill University in Montreal, she attended the University of Pennsylvania in Philadelphia where she received her Ph.D.

Her publications and research are centered in seventeenth-century French literature and culture. Her two books on Corneille were published by Droz in 1962 and 1977. Articles dealing with various genres and representative authors have appeared in scholarly journals here and abroad. Two thematic studies on women characters from classical to Renaissance and seventeenth-century literature have appeared in the last few years.

She received a Camargo Foundation grant for 1986 to work on a study of Racine's plays.

Preface

The aim of this study is to bring to the English-speaking public, especially to the academic community, an easy-to-consult, well-documented and concise volume on La Fontaine and his works that includes consideration of the historical, social, and cultural background in which the poet lived, and on the scholarship and criticism these works have generated in the last twenty-five or thirty years.

The students and the general public will find, we hope, a useful and stimulating introduction to La Fontaine's life and works: more advanced scholars will find resource material for further investigation in the notes and bibliography.

La Fontaine is a great poet who has become a "classic": his *Fables,* on which his reputation rests, are part of the literary canon of French writers and are studied in schools. His other works, however, have been rediscovered and are the object of quite a few recent studies. We have therefore given to *Adonis,* the *Contes,* and *Psyché* the attention they deserve. *Adonis,* the subject of a celebrated essay by the poet Paul Valéry, and representative of the short and brilliant court life at Vaux, foreshadows many of the later masterpieces and already contains the major themes developed in the *Fables.* We have also indicated some of the most important reevaluations and interpretations that have been proposed in recent scholarship.

In presenting the *Fables,* a selective process was necessary. Our choice was guided by several considerations: we have naturally discussed the anthologized fables, most frequently studied in literature courses. We have also included those illustrating La Fontaine's personality and taste, his attitudes toward humanity and society, and his views about his art and literature in general.

The abundance of scholarly investigation in the past few decades testifies to the importance of La Fontaine's works and to his secure position as one of the greatest French poets of all time.

We hope this modest volume will help many readers to a better, fuller understanding of his versatility, his extraordinary range of interests, his delightful sense of humor, and the richness and flavor of his language.

Marie-Odile Sweetser

University of Illinois at Chicago

Acknowledgments

It is a pleasure to acknowledge the support and help received from the following institution, learned societies, and individuals:

The University of Illinois at Chicago named me a Senior Fellow in its Institute for the Humanities in 1983.

The Association internationale des études françaises and its executive director, Professor Robert Garapon of the Sorbonne, welcomed my study "Le Jardin: nature et culture chez La Fontaine" at its 1981 annual meeting.

The Société d'Etude du XVIIe siècle invited me to present a paper at its international colloquium in Paris in March 1983, presided over by Professors Roland Mousnier and Jean Mesnard and sponsored by the Centre national de la recherche scientifique.

The North American Society for Seventeenth Century French Literature and its president for 1983, Professor Bernard Beugnot, invited me to chair one of the sessions of the 1983 annual conference at the University of Montreal on "Voyages. Récits et imaginaire."

The University of Illinois at Chicago librarians helped me in my research: Professor Robert Daugherty, Head of Circulation; past and present humanities bibliographers, Professors Peter Clark, Frank Imler, John Cullars, and their dedicated staff.

My colleague at UIC, Professor David O'Connell, field editor for French of the Twayne World Authors series, kindly suggested that having been raised on La Fontaine's *Fables* and having taught them in seventeenth-century French literature courses, I should undertake this study. He has closely followed its progress and made useful and welcome suggestions.

Professor Richard Danner of Ohio University was most kind in providing galley proofs of his important new book *Patterns of Irony in La Fontaine's Fables*.

Professor John L. Logan of the Pennsylvania State University lent me a copy of his Yale dissertation on *Psyché*.

Professor David Lee Rubin of the University of Virginia, guest editor of the La Fontaine issue for *L'Esprit créateur*, Winter 1981, welcomed my study on *Adonis*.

Professor Philip A. Wadsworth kindly provided bibliographical information.

My husband, Franklin P. Sweetser, has been most helpful in the task of proofreading.

Last, but not least, Mrs. Pam Jurkowski, who has done the word processing of the manuscript, has shown great patience, care for details, and cheerfulness.

To all my sincere and deeply felt gratitude.

Editions Used and Abbreviations

Quotations from the works of La Fontaine are from the following editions and are cited in the text by the abbreviated titles indicated:

Oeuvres complètes. Edited by Jean Marmier. Préface by Pierre Clarac. Paris: Seuil, L'Intégrale, 1965. Cited as *O.C.*

Oeuvres diverses. Edited by Pierre Clarac. Paris: Gallimard, Pléiade, 1958. Cited as *O.D.*

Contes et nouvelles en vers. Edited by Nicole Ferrier and Jean-Pierre Collinet. Paris: Garnier-Flammarion, 1980. Cited as *Contes.*

Fables choisies mises en vers. Edited by Georges Couton. Paris: Garnier, 1962. Cited as *Fables.*

For uniformity's sake, quotations in English of the *Fables* are taken from the translation by Marianne Moore, *The Fables of La Fontaine* (New York: Viking Press, 1954). All other translations from French into English are my own, except where noted.

Chronology

1662   Elégie "Aux Nymphes de Vaux" published anonymously.

1663   "Ode au Roi," appeal to the king for clemency. La Fontaine accompanies his uncle Jannart in his exile to Limoges: letters to his wife will become *Relation d'un voyage de Paris en Limousin,* not published during La Fontaine's lifetime.

1664   La Fontaine enters the household of the dowager duchesse d'Orléans, Madame, widow of Gaston d'Orléans, brother of Louis XIII at the Luxembourg palace.

1665   *Contes et nouvelles en vers,* part 1.

1666   *Contes et nouvelles en vers,* part 2.

1668   *Fables choisies mises en vers,* dedicated to the dauphin, son of Louis XIV, born in 1661. Books 1–6.

1669   *Les Amours de Psyché et de Cupidon,* dedicated to the duchesse de Bouillon. With it, is published a revised version of *Adonis.*

1671   *Contes et nouvelles en vers,* part 3. Dedication to the Prince de Conti of the *Recueil de poésies chrétiennes et diverses.*

1672   Death of the dowager duchesse d'Orléans.

1673   La Fontaine becomes guest of Madame de La Sablière. "Poème de la captivité de saint Malc," dedicated to the Cardinal de Bouillon.

1674   *Daphné,* libretto for an opera, refused by Lulli; hence *Le Florentin,* satire against Lulli.

1678–1679   *Fables choisies mises en vers,* with five additional books, 7–11, dedicated to Madame de Montespan.

1682   "Le Poème du Quinquina," dedicated to the duchesse de Bouillon.
Birth of the duc de Bourgogne, grandson of Louis XIV.

1683   La Fontaine elected to the Académie française to replace Colbert. Louis XIV postpones La Fontaine's reception.

1684   2 May, Reception of La Fontaine at the Académie française: "Discours à Madame de La Sablière."

1685   *Ouvrages de prose et de poésie des sieurs de Maucroix et de La Fontaine,* two volumes. Contains new *contes,* fables, and other pieces.

1687   "Epître à Huet." Beginning of the "Querelle des Anciens et des Modernes."

1691   *Astrée, tragédie lyrique,* libretto by La Fontaine, music by Colasse, son-in-law of Lulli.

1693   Death of Madame de La Sablière. La Fontaine becomes the guest of d'Hervart.
        Fables choisies, book 12, dedicated to the duc de Bourgogne.

1695   Death of La Fontaine.

Chapter One
Beginnings

Very little is known about the early part of Jean de La Fontaine's life. The house where the poet was born in Château-Thierry, a small provincial town in Champagne, some fifty miles northeast of Paris, still exists but has known many changes in the course of the centuries. It is now a municipal museum. Documents for the first twenty years of the writer's life are scarce.[1]

His baptism was entered in the parish of Saint-Crépin register on 8 July 1621. According to the custom of the period, it probably means that Jean de La Fontaine was born a day or two earlier. He was the son of Charles de La Fontaine, "King's Councillor," "Maître des Eaux et Forêts," a government official supervising royal domains, and Françoise Pidoux, from a good family from Poitou. Her father had been physician to Kings Henri III and Henri IV. She was a widow when she married Charles de La Fontaine and had a daughter from her first marriage, Anne de Jouy. A son, Claude, was born to the La Fontaines two years later in September 1623.

The education and formative years of young La Fontaine are not documented. Most biographers state that, in all likelihood, he attended Château-Thierry "collège," a secondary institution where humanities were taught to the sons of the middle class.[2] The curriculum, revised at the beginning of the seventeenth century, included Latin and some Greek and was meant to prepare young men for the law and for administrative and judicial positions. D'Olivet, who with Pellisson wrote the first *History of the French Academy*, claims that La Fontaine learned Latin only, because he was educated at a provincial institution.[3] Nevertheless, the collège of Château-Thierry had an excellent reputation.

It is possible but not proven that the brothers Maucroix, Louis and François, from the neighboring town of Noyon attended the collège of Château-Thierry. Nineteenth-century scholars record the existence of a book, now lost, that would indicate that Jean de La Fontaine and François de Maucroix knew each other in school. It was a textbook of selected *Dialogs of Lucian*, a Greek text with Latin translation on the facing page,[4] that bore the name, crossed out, of the older brother, Ludovicus Maucroix. On the inside blank page was written: "De la Fontaine, nice boy, very quiet and unassuming." It was customary that a schoolbook would be passed from an older to a younger brother. The book may have been in the hands of François when La Fontaine wrote his name on two of its pages. This may indicate that even if La Fontaine did not become proficient or fluent in Greek, the language was taught at the collège of Château-Thierry: the poet may have had at least some basic training through contact with the selected texts used in teaching.[5]

Some scholars doubt that, in later life, at least, La Fontaine was able to read any Greek text in the original. Noémi Hepp, in her magisterial thesis, commenting on La Fontaine's line "Homère et son rival sont mes Dieux du Parnasse"[6](Homer and his rival [Virgil] are my poetic gods), states that La Fontaine did not know Greek.[7] Later on, discussing La Fontaine's unfinished tragedy *Achille*, she notes: "La Fontaine loved Homer, although he could not read it in the original," and quotes the testimonies of Louis Racine and Madame Dacier.[8] The fact that Madame Dacier read to La Fontaine her translation of Homer and that Racine gave to the poet a Latin translation of Homer may mean that La Fontaine had forgotten the rudiments of Greek learned as a schoolboy, as was often the case, according to the educator and hellenist Rollin.[9]

One of the foremost La Fontaine scholars, Pierre Clarac, mentions another instance that raises the question whether the poet read Plato and Plutarch, his favorite authors in later life, in the original or in a Latin or French translation. Pierre Clarac quotes a letter of 29 May 1680 to the prince de Condé,[10] sending him a translation of the beginning of one of Plato's dialogs by La Fontaine. The specialist surmises that if the poet undertook such a translation, even with the help of his friend Maucroix and a Latin translation, he must have possessed some knowledge of Greek.[11]

It is generally acknowledged that after studying in Château-Thierry until he was fourteen or fifteen, that is for the first four years of the humanities curriculum, he completed his studies in a "collège"in Paris where he apparently had as classmate the future writer Antoine Furetière.[12] In 1652, the latter signed an official paper, stating that he had known Jean de La Fontaine for more than sixteen years, having gone to school and maintained friendly relations with him afterwards.[13] This document, which testified to the good character of an office seeker, was required for La Fontaine's purchase of the position of "Maître particulier triennal des eaux et forêts," which made him a government official in charge of royal domains. Since Furetière was born and raised in Paris, it is assumed that he went to school in the capital. La Fontaine therefore must have been his classmate in a Parisian "collège."

His admission to the Congrégation de l'Oratoire on 27 April 1641 at the house of the Oratorians on rue St-Honoré was recorded in the yearbook of the order. His younger brother Claude, who joined him in October 1641, left the order in 1650 but remained in the religious life. The Oratoire was one of the new orders, founded by Cardinal de Bérulle in 1611, that contributed to the Catholic revival of the late sixteenth, early seventeenth century known as the Counter-Reformation.

The life of a novice at the Oratoire was quite structured. It is difficult to imagine how the young La Fontaine would have adapted to it. He seemed to have had trouble both with the rigorous schedule and with the study of theology. But he was befriended by one of the members of the order, Father Desmares, who tried to teach him some theology. According to an anecdote published in the eighteenth century, La Fontaine said to friends who asked him what he did at the Oratoire: "Desmares had fun reading Saint Augustine and I the *Astrée*."[14] Saint Augustine was one of the early fathers of the church whose writings were very much studied by seventeenth-century theologians, especially the Jansenists.[15] L'*Astrée*, which La Fontaine read with such delight, is the lengthy pastoral novel by Honoré d'Urfé (1607–27) that had an immense success throughout the century and after. La Fontaine, like many well-educated society men and women, loved novels and expressed his enduring taste in a charming *ballade* (*O.D.*, 585–86; *O.C.*, 191–92) the refrain of which is: "I do enjoy love stories." He was a voracious reader of fiction from the Greek romance by Heliodorus to those of seventeenth-century French novelists, La Calprenède, Gomberville, and the Scudérys, including medieval chivalric romances, sixteenth-century prose by Rabelais and others, and popular short stories.

With such tastes, it is not surprising that young La Fontaine's religious vocation did not last very long. It is not known whether he withdrew from the Oratoire on his own or was told by his superiors that he was not suited to the monastic life. His stay there does reveal, however, that an important aspect of his personality was a leaning toward meditative retreat and internal reflexion. It helps to understand the religious side of his poetic works and his association with translators of Saint Augustine and with pious persons, Christians of Jansenist leaning.

After leaving the Oratoire, La Fontaine went back to Château-Thierry where he had the leisure that allowed him to read his favorite authors, poets and novelists. Among the poets, he certainly knew well Ovid, Horace, and Virgil, as the allusions and creative imitations found in his poetry show;[16] among the French poets, Malherbe, Racan, most probably Tristan—although La Fontaine never mentioned the latter.[16] Théophile and Voiture were by this time quite famous, and La Fontaine must have read their work too. According to Jean-Pierre Chauveau, it is probably Voiture and the society poets that had the greatest influence on his style in the early part of his career.[17]

His poetic vocation was born, according to an anecdote recounted by d'Olivet, when he heard an officer, quartered in Château-Thierry, give an inspired reading of an ode by Malherbe: "Que direz-vous, races futures . . ." (What will you say, future generations . . .). Young La Fontaine "listened to this ode with obvious pleasure, admiration and awe. He started immediately to read Malherbe. . . . It did not take long for him to want to follow in his footsteps."[18] The fact that throughout his literary career La Fontaine considered Malherbe as a master is well documented, from the early fable "Le Meunier, son fils et l'âne" (3,1) to the "Epître à Huet" (1687).

Malherbe (1555–1628) was a "modern" poet who had reacted strongly against the poetic concepts and style of the Renaissance and of the generation that followed the recognized masters of the Pléiade, Ronsard and Du Bellay. His *Commentaires sur Desportes*, critical remarks on the works of that late sixteenth-century poet, are considered as the expression of his own doctrine and as foreshadowing the aesthetic principles of classicism. La Fontaine admired, as did many others, the solid structure, the density and purity of Malherbe's verse, but with the true independence of genius he did not imitate him, but created instead a freer, more flexible poetic style.

Among La Fontaine specialists, a lively controversy still exists about the identity of the first "master" whom La Fontaine later repudiated, finding his style was too ornate, and the date when this repudiation took place.[19] The passage of the "Epître à Huet" mentioning this brilliant but dangerous master reads as follows:

> Je pris certain auteur autrefois pour mon maître;
> Il pensa me gâter. A la fin, grâce aux Cieux,
> Horace, par bonheur, me dessilla les yeux
> L'auteur avait du bon, du meilleur; et la France
> Estimait dans ses vers le tour et la cadence.
> Qui ne les eût prisés? J'en demeurai ravi;
> Mais ses traits ont perdu quiconque l'a suivi.
> Son trop d'esprit s'épand en trop de belles choses:
> Tous métaux y sont or, toutes fleurs y sont roses.
>   (*O.D.*, 648; *O.C.*, 493).

> (In my youth, I chose a certain author as my master
> He almost spoiled my style. At last, thanks to Heaven
> Horace, fortunately opened my eyes.
> The author was among the best; and France
> Esteemed in his verse the style and the rhythm.
> Who would not have liked them? I was delighted with them
> But his concetti have ruined anyone who imitated him.
> His exaggerated cleverness is carried over into too many beautiful
>   things.
> All metals are gold, all flowers roses in his verse.)

The last line, a quote from a poem by Malherbe brought d'Olivet to the conclusion that Malherbe came to seem too ornate to La Fontaine who leaned toward a more natural expression. A note by La Fontaine states, however, that the *concetti* were favored by poets who came immediately after Malherbe, that is by the *précieux* of the 1640s. Pierre Clarac in his note to this passage suggests Voiture; according to him, La Fontaine's comment excludes Malherbe (*O.D.*, n. 20, 989–90).

In d'Olivet's anecdote, a certain Pintrel, relative of the poet, described as "full of good sense and well educated", advised young La Fontaine to read the Latin poets, Horace, Virgil, and Terence as models of classical, elegant, refined, but restrained poetic diction. The advice seemed to have born fruit since La Fontaine's first published literary work was an adaptation of Terence's *Eunuch*.

From these wide-ranging readings, one can infer that young La

Fontaine was equally well versed in classical writings, which he read in Latin, and in the vernacular literature. The coexistence and successful blending of the two cultures in his own work is an important feature of French classicism. It combines on one hand the culture of lawyers and scholars, based on the Latin humanistic training received in the Jesuit and Oratorian "collèges"; on the other, the worldly culture of aristocratic society—ladies who did not know Latin, gentlemen who had received a military training, not a scholarly one. They read and enjoyed novels, poetry, and plays in French and shared the taste of the lower classes for the supernatural found in medieval romances and fairy tales.[20]

It was fitting for a son of the well-to-do, educated, and ambitious middle class to study law, in order to prepare for an administrative or judicial career: Corneille and Molière had taken that course before La Fontaine. While studying law, he met other students and friends in a literary circle, the *académie,* at Paul Pellisson's house where he had social contacts with various writers and scholars. Pellisson (1624–93) played an important part in the cultural life that centered around Nicolas Fouquet, "surintendant des finances" and a generous patron of the arts, whose trusted assistant and secretary he became in 1652.[21] Various historians believe that it was Pellisson and his friend Mademoiselle de Scudéry who introduced La Fontaine into Fouquet's circle some ten years later. La Fontaine, while a student in Paris, also met Gédéon and François Tallemant, Olivier Patru, Conrart, Antoine de La Sablière, and Jean Chapelain (*Recueil,* 37).

In November 1647, a marriage contract was signed at La Ferté-Milon, a town not far from Château-Thierry and home of the bride, between Jean de La Fontaine and Marie Héricart who was only fourteen and a half years old. She was the daughter of Louis Héricart, "lieutenant civil et criminel", police commissioner of the township, and Agnès Petit. According to the contract, Jean was to inherit his father's official position of "Maître des eaux et forêts." In the *ancien régime,* the royal government sold "offices" which brought to the holder an annual income and were usually transmissible. La Fontaine was also to receive a sum of ten thousand pounds and properties valued at twelve thousand pounds. The bride was given thirty thousand pounds as an advance payment of her inheritance. From these figures, one can see that the two families belonged to the well-to-do middle class and that the poet and his bride were contracting a suitable socioeconomic match.

The age and character differences between the two have often been noted by historians who examined the relationship between the poet and his wife.[22] According to Tallemant des Réaux, a seventeenth-century writer and habitué of the salons, the marriage was La Fontaine's father's idea. The young man agreed to please his father who wanted to see his son settled. Tallemant, considered by some as a rather malicious gossip, by others as well informed, writes in one of his *Historiettes* about the couple:

His wife says he is such a dreamer that he sometimes forgets for three weeks that he is married. She is a flirt who has not behaved very well lately, but that does not bother him. People tell him "but so and so flirts with your wife"—"Goodness," he replies, "let him try as much as he can, it does not bother me. He will get tired of her as I did." This indifference drives her mad, she gets worked up about it, as for him, he finds love wherever he can. When an abbess retired in town, he offered her lodgings. One day his wife came upon them by surprise. He just stopped short, bowed to her and left.[23]

La Fontaine's marriage should be considered in the perspective of seventeenth-century French mores. Marriage was not based on a romantic concept of love but on a community of family interests. La Fontaine's apparent indifference towards his wife and his casual affairs were not uncommon. An easygoing, tolerant attitude in those matters was expected from well-bred, civilized people. Philip Wadsworth sums up extremely well the La Fontaine's matrimonial situation: "their marriage worked out reasonably well. . . . They made occasional trips to Paris, staying at the house of Marie's uncle, Jacques Jannart who was an influential lawyer and close associate of Nicolas Fouquet, La Fontaine's first important literary patron. One can imagine that the poet watched over his wife's education or at least joined her in the reading of novels, her favorite literary fare—for she became a woman of some culture and refinement and even a sort of provincial *femme savante*."[24] Some historians depict her as a *précieuse* or a "blue stocking." She did preside over a literary circle in Château-Thierry. In a 1662 letter, her relative, playwright Jean Racine, asks La Fontaine for his opinion, as well as that of his wife and their circle on some verse he had composed.

A son, Charles, was born to them in 1653. Apparently La Fontaine paid little attention to him, and he has been described as not fond of children. This observation is based on remarks found in the *Fables,*

"Mais un fripon d'enfant, cet âge est sans pitié," ("Les Deux Pigeons," 9, 2, *Fables,* 247; But a naughty boy, this age does not know pity), about a boy who tried to kill with his sling a wandering dove, and the disparaging remarks about the schoolboy who was stealing fruit and ruining the blossoms of fruit trees in his neighbor's garden ("L'Ecolier, le pédant, et le maître d'un jardin," 9, 5, *Fables,* 250–51). Philip Wadsworth (83) attributes La Fontaine's lack of attention to his wife and son at that time to the preparation of his first published work, *L'Eunuque,* the adaptation of Terence's comedy, which appeared in 1654. To be sure, the poet must have become absorbed in modifying the original to eliminate its prostitution and rape, unacceptable themes for a mid-seventeenth-century audience, accustomed to decorum. In the French adaptation, the lovers are presented according to the classical conventions: their love quest ends in marriage. While acknowledging the part played by literary conventions, Wadsworth "sees in *L'Eunuque* some faint echoes from La Fontaine's own life—the period of courtship and the first happy years of marriage" (85). His first attempt at literature was a failure, however; La Fontaine had not yet found his own personal, inimitable voice.

Wadsworth also stresses that La Fontaine maintained some form of family life with frequent trips to Château-Thierry for almost twenty-five years. It was after 1673 that the poet lived in Paris, as a guest of Madame de La Sablière. Did he have any qualms about his unconventional life? Maybe so, if one reads personal innuendoes in the 1685 poem, "Philémon et Baucis," included later in book 12 of the *Fables.* The old couple presents an idealized image of lasting conjugal love: "Il s'aiment jusqu'au bout, malgré l'effort des ans. / Ah! si. . . . Mais autre part j'ai porté mes présents." ("Philémon et Baucis," 12, 25, *Fables,* 360; They loved each other until the end, in spite of the destructive years. / Ah! if. . . . But I have taken my presents elsewhere / [Elsewhere: not in the temple of conjugal fidelity]).

From her portrait, attributed to the well-known painter of the period, Pierre Mignard (reproduced in Pierre Clarac, *La Fontaine par lui-même,* 41 and in *O.C.,* 10), Marie Héricart looks like a handsome woman "of dignity and breeding . . . with an attractive but angular face and an expression of resignation or sadness in her large dark eyes" (92). She must have possessed a certain sense of humor and some understanding and indulgence for her husband's ways, according to the letters he wrote her while accompanying her uncle Jannart in his exile in Limousin in 1663.[25] To be sure, they were not intimate letters, but were intended to be read by their friends in their literary circle of Château-Thierry. The poet, in these charming letters, teases his wife about her liking for chivalric romances and the adventures of their heroes. He fears therefore that the account of his trip will appear somewhat dull and prosaic in comparison, so he will try to liven matters up: "C'est à moi de les assaisonner, si je puis, en telle sorte qu'elles vous plaisent; et c'est à vous de louer en cela mon intention, quand elle ne serait pas suivie du succès." (*O.D.,* 533; *O.C.,* 17; It is up to me to spice them up, if I can, so that they entertain you; it is up to you to praise my good intentions, even if they were not successful.) The letters include frequent allusions to women met on the trip; the tone is playful, the encounters mildly flirtatious: his wife and friends were to take these "adventures" as a joke: the writer makes fun of himself, of his lighthearted but harmless attraction for pretty women. Wadsworth concludes: "but these artistic preoccupations do not prevent the letters from having a certain warmth and tenderness. He took the trouble to write them and he enjoyed making fun of his wife's rather precious tastes. . . . The letters demonstrate that La Fontaine, although perhaps an unconventional and unsatisfactory husband, was still a rather affectionate one" (88).

The poet was not a model husband, but the way he treated his wife did not, it would seem, stem from unkindness, scorn, or cruelty, but rather from his congenital disposition and basic nature: he found it impossible to limit his interest to one person, or one subject; he needed variety, diversion, stimulation, excitement, dreams, poetry. The steady, limited life and career of a government official devoted to his professional duties and his family were not for him. This did not mean that he did not have sincere and warm feelings for members of his family. But he was aware of his inability to adjust to conventional standards and described himself accurately, if again with some lighthearted self-mockery, in his light verse: "Epitaphe d'un paresseux" ("Epitaph for a lazy man," referring to himself, *O.D.,* 495–596; *O.C.,* 459); in his *Elégies* in which he presents himself as a man suffering from the pangs of unrequited love (*O.C.,* 478–81; *O.D.,* 601–09); and above all in his famous

"Discours à Madame de La Sablière," read during his reception by the French Academy on 2 May 1684, perhaps with some wistfulness, if not some self-reproach, "Papillon du Parnasse" (Poetic Butterfly):

> Je vais de fleur en fleur et d'objet en objet;
> A beaucoup de plaisirs je mêle un peu de gloire.
> J'irais plus haut peut-être au temple de Mémoire
> Si dans un genre seul j'avais usé mes jours;
> Mais quoi! je suis volage en vers comme en amours.
>   (*O.D.*, 645–46; *O.C.*, 491)

> (I go from flower to flower, from one object of love to another.
> To many pleasures, I add a little reputation.
> I would go higher perhaps in the temple of Fame
> If in one genre only I had spent my life
> But after all I am flighty in verse as in love.)

This desire for fame was not fulfilled by La Fontaine's first attempt in the literary field: his comedy *L'Eunuque* was neither performed nor noticed. But apparently the poet was not discouraged from pursuing an elusive fame. The assertion that he cultivated many genres was going to be documented by an extremely varied literary production.

Chapter Two

The Vaux Period

In his anecdotes about La Fontaine, the seventeenth-century gossip writer, Tallemant des Réaux, brings up, besides the amorous propensities of the poet and the neglect shown to his wife, his absentmindedness: he was "un grand resveur"; he lived in another world. That penchant for daydreaming found the perfect outlet in the fairy-tale setting of Vaux, Fouquet's estate, the center of a brilliant court life. Antoine Adam, the editor of Tallemant's *Historiettes* underlines the interest of this portrait since, at the time it was written in 1656–57, La Fontaine was not yet famous, his legend had not been established: the observations are therefore reliable.[1] These remarks confirm later views of La Fontaine as an original, a dreamer not in contact with the realities of life.

In 1658, Charles de La Fontaine, father of the poet, died, leaving a rather complicated estate to be settled, and his offspring burdened with debts. His older son, Jean, inherited his *offices*, his official positions, "capitaine des chasses au duché de Château-Thierry" and "maître particulier ancien des eaux et forêts." They were added to another *office* acquired in 1652 by the poet. Jean's brother Claude renounced his share of the paternal estate, provided the older brother would pay him a flat sum of 8,225 pounds, 6,400 as a down payment, the remainder to be reimbursed in three parts within fifteen months. All his life, La Fontaine was plagued with financial problems and had to find generous patrons.

One does not know the exact date or circumstances of his introduction to the powerful Surintendant des Finances, Nicolas Fouquet. Some historians have suggested that the writer Pellisson, who was Fouquet's protégé and personal secretary, introduced La Fontaine to the surintendant. He was recruiting writers and artists to enhance his patron's presige. Others think that La Fontaine's uncle by marriage, the lawyer Jacques Jannart, employed by Fouquet in his legal capacities, was responsible for the introduction.[2] In any case, that person opened the doors of opportunity to the poet.

In his brief and unequaled career as patron of the arts after the Fronde, the Surintendant des Finances Nicolas Fouquet 1615–1680 brought together the most brilliant group of French artists that had ever been assembled in the kingdom: the poet La Fontaine, the playwright Molière, the architect Le Vau, the landscape gardener Le Nôtre and the painter Le Brun. . . . Following the example of the Italian princes of the High Renaissance, Fouquet acted as if he wanted to endow the official exercise of patronage with the charm of private patronage as practiced by noble lords in opposition to Richelieu's. . . . After Mazarin's death one of the first decisive acts of Louis XIV was the disgrace of Fouquet, following which Louis placed in the service of the crown most of the artists the Surintendant had sponsored.[3]

Most historians agree that the surintendant Nicolas Fouquet was an important patron who left his mark on literature and the arts, as well as on the political history of France from the end of the Fronde until his arrest on 5 September 1661 by order of young king Louis XIV.[4] Towards the middle of the seventeenth-century, the values of the old, feudal aristocracy and those of the new nobility, the *robe,* converged in an ideal of the patron who attracted high officials. Clergy, princes, nobles, members of the high courts, the *parlements,* ministers of state felt it was their duty, their social obligation to support arts and letters and even historiography. Upstarts and social climbers in particular attempted to strengthen their position through patronage and a relationship of an almost mystical nature was created between protector and protégé, as in the case of Fouquet and Pellisson.[5] From 1657 on, the writer and his friend Madeleine de Scudéry, a well-known novelist and hostess of a literary salon, were part of the surintendant's establishment and advised him about his patronage policy.[6] Numerous fashionable poets and a few great writers came into the orbit of their master, and praised his talents and generosity in flattering dedicatory remarks. The writers destined to greatness were La Fontaine, Corneille, and Molière; the most famous works commissioned by Fouquet were Corneille's tragedy *Oedipe* (1659), preceded by a verse epistle praising his patron, and Molière's comedy *Les Fâcheux,* which received its first performance at Vaux for the lavish festivities offered by Fouquet to young king Louis XIV on 17 August 1661. La Fontaine described the festivities in his letter to his friend Maucroix (*O.D.,* 522–27), stressing the new, elegant, natural style of Molière's comedy, a far cry from the old farcical, popular manner (*O.D.,* 525–26). The brilliance of the festivities probably made a strong impression on the king, who could not tolerate being overshadowed by a subject; hence Fouquet's arrest and the subsequent hiring by Louis of Fouquet's team of artists.

There seems to have existed a cultural and aesthetic climate at the court of Vaux, representing the taste and interests of a new generation. Fouquet, during the short years of his power, had shown, according to Pellisson, a well-informed love for letters and the arts and an essential quality that must have been a factor in the case of La Fontaine, a free spirit: "Fouquet respected the freedom of authors, allowing them free rein in bringing their talents and genius into flower."[7]

Whatever may have been the talent or genius of a writer in the seventeenth century, the necessity of acquiring powerful protectors, of pleasing them, and of obtaining the approbation of both the court and Paris society remained an inescapable fact. La Fontaine wrote light, occasional verse for Fouquet and his wife. The most important works written for Fouquet by our poet were, however, the sumptuous mythological poem *Adonis* and the fragments destined to be an unfinished piece praising Fouquet's domain, *Le Songe de Vaux*.

The stature of *Adonis* is now well established: the great French poet Paul Valéry, in his justly celebrated essay, first published in 1921, "Au sujet d'*Adonis*," analyzed convincingly La Fontaine's genius in this first major piece, as well as in later works.[8] He provided brilliant insights about a poetic mind at work.

Adonis was presented to Fouquet in a beautiful calligraphic manuscript by Nicolas Jarry, with a frontispiece by François Chauveau, during the summer of 1658. Eleven years later, after Fouquet's condemnation to life imprisonment, a second version was published with *Les Amours de Psyché et de Cupidon,* which is generally considered as an outgrowth of the Vaux period. The second version was without the dedication to Fouquet, for obvious reasons. The lines referring to La Fontaine's former patron were replaced by an invocation to Aminte, a woman the poet was wooing, and several stylistic changes were made in individual lines. It was published again in 1671, with slight corrections, following the *Fables nouvelles.* The text published in modern editions is that of the last version revised by the author, according to generally accepted standards of modern editing, where the original version of a text is often considered of importance only for historical or aesthetic reasons.

In the dedication of the manuscript of 1658, which represents the original version of *Adonis,* La Fontaine indulges in the customary flattery: he discerns in the person of the surintendant the statesman, the man of taste, the *honnête homme,* and the minister who has shown himself to be a worthy successor to Richelieu (*O.D.,* 798). The poet, in an encomiastic style that makes systematic use of hyperbole, presents his patron as the "hero" who will put an end to the dark ages. The memory of the civil wars and their ravages remained very vivid in the minds of the French people in 1658. If Henry IV had succeeded in achieving a brief period of peace, prosperity, and justice after the religious wars, the troubles that arose during two difficult regencies—that of Marie de Médicis after Henry's assassination in 1610 and that of Anne of Austria after Louis XIII's death in 1643, when the kingdom was torn apart by the Fronde from 1648 to 1652—had left a deep impression, a horror of civil disorders and rebellion in the young Louis XIV as well as in his subjects. A leading La Fontaine scholar proposes aptly an allegorical reading of *Adonis:* like the hero of the poem, who had slain a monster, Fouquet is proposed as a conqueror of ignorance.[9] One could also see in the monster the disturber of civil peace, and the minister of state as the victor over the monster of civil war. In his trial, Fouquet traded on this idea, evoking the services rendered and his loyalty to the monarchy during the Fronde.[10] The poem envisages the minister as a new Maecenas, who will guarantee a golden age in which the young king will be Augustus and in which the Muses will reign.

The affection for Fouquet attributed to the Muses transforms him into an object of love, just as the hero of the poem, Adonis, becomes the object of love of Venus, goddess and mother of Eros. The theme chosen by the poet is therefore fitting, for it suits the recipient's public image. The poem becomes a monument erected to the goddess of love and her lover and to the glory of the poet's patron. The human and contemporary level is linked to the mythical one by the mediation of the Muses who inspire poets: the latter love to acquire a reputation for themselves, but can also bestow it upon those to whom their works are dedicated. Moreover, La Fontaine, before *Psyché,* the *Contes,* and the *Fables,* allows us here a glimpse of his humor through his amused skepticism: he removes Venus from her pedestal, presents her on a human level as an attractive flirt, full of devil-may-care, "elle qui n'avait pas accoutumé de jeter des larmes pour la perte de ses amants" (*O.D.,* 798; she who was not used to shedding tears over the loss of her lovers). The dedication thus enjoins the minister to relax, to let himself be charmed by a beautiful love story, without taking its tragic ending too seriously. The poet is already providing to his protector and his court "le plaisir des larmes" (the pleasure of shedding tears), as he will in *Psyché:*[11] the pleasure, too, of a delicate irony, of a veiled humor, capable of leading the attentive reader well beyond the events of the narrative, towards the eternal questions of life, love, and death.

The love felt by a goddess for a simple but attractive mortal correlates to the love of the Muses for the recipient of the poem. According to gossip, Fouquet had also been favored by some brilliant society women. Yet, beyond the flattering conquests due to his fortune and power, Fouquet had inspired lasting feelings of loyalty and friendship that were to persist during his disgrace. It is well known how faithfully Pellisson, Mademoiselle de Scudéry, Madame de Sévigné,[12] and La Fontaine himself tried to defend him: the minister was worthy of love; a love poem could only have pleased him. Traditionally in literary allusion the powerful gods and demigods of mythology—Jupiter, Apollo, Hercules—and the conquerors, Alexander and Caesar, were reserved for kings.[13] So, the choice of a beautiful love story by La Fontaine for Fouquet was wise, since it avoided any possible royal jealousy.[14]

In the invocation of 1658, the poet gave full praise to the professional, mathematical, and legal qualifications of his patron as well as to his discriminating taste (*O.D.,* 800, n. 5). He claimed there was an intimate harmony of taste between patron and poet, the voluptuous sweetness and ornamental style of the poem recalling those of Vaux.[15] The theme of happy, idyllic love in a bucolic retreat, which is that of the first part of *Adonis,* is found throughout La Fontaine's works, from *Les Amours de Psyché et de Cupidon* to the last fables.[16]

The care with which La Fontaine revised his poem for the second version of 1669 shows clearly how much the work meant to him.[17] The love theme, both in the invocation and in the poem itself is even more strongly orchestrated, with an implied mirror effect, Aminte being invited to emulate Venus, whom she resembles by her beauty and charm.[18] Love blossoms most naturally, most spontaneously between two creatures equal in charm and beauty, despite differences, as the goddess seeks out a mere mortal: "—Amour rend ses sujets égaux, lui dit-elle." (*O.D.,* 7; Love makes his subjects equal, she said to him). Their happiness is perfect in its simplicity and complete reciprocity: "Quelles sont les douceurs qu'en ces bois ils goûtèrent!" (*O.D.*, 7; What sweet delights they enjoyed in these woods!). But it is worldly preoccupations, duties imposed by society, fear of gossip and concern for her reputation that compel Venus to leave this retreat, to destroy this ineffable happiness.[19] The superior happiness of a loving couple is celebrated in still more direct fashion, but using nevertheless the idyllic tone of pastoral conventions in the famous lyrical meditation that concludes the fable "Les Deux Pigeons:"

> Fond lovers, since love is all in all, if you go away,
> Come hastening home again:
> Each a beautiful world to the other of the two,
> Forever strange, forever new.
> Love the world in each of you, unaware of all the rest.[20]

Venus sacrifices her lover and their happiness, to society. He, in his sadness and loneliness, seeks a diversion to his sorrow:

> Enfin, pour divertir l'ennui qui le possède,
> On lui dit que la chasse est un puissant remède.
>
> (*O.D.*, 10)

> (Finally, to dispel the sorrow that takes hold of him
> He is told that hunting is a powerful cure.)

The poet here introduces, with a light, indulgent irony, a reflection on the weakness of human nature, a weakness that Pascal endows with tragic irony.[21] It is also very probably a reminiscence of the *Remedia amoris* of Ovid (ll. 199–212) whose *Metamorphoses* La Fontaine had used as a source of his poem. But on a more profound level, the similarity with Pascal is revealing: Epicurean and Augustinian doctrines come together in their analysis of human nature, although they differ in other ways.[22]

This basic human inability to know how to recognize and preserve happiness, to cultivate self-knowledge and peace of soul and heart, is one of the deeper themes of *Les Amours de Psyché et de Cupidon* and of the *Fables*. Adonis, forsaken by the one who had singled him out from all other mortals, abandons in his turn the sole pursuit that ought to be his, that of love. In seeking forgetfulness and distraction, he gives up his fidelity to the cult of love. One can see in this attitude an idealized, precious concept of love, in harmony with the taste of the salons, of the court of Vaux where Pellisson and Mademoiselle de Scudéry played an important role. A Platonic concept seems to be suggested concerning Adonis who knows "ecstasy through a revelation of the beauty which takes him out of himself and raises him to the divine." His mistake, which will have a tragic consequence, consists precisely in forgetting this ecstasy, in falling back from the divine world of love into the human and mundane world of the hunt. As for Venus, she "descends from heaven, but she is also a 'daughter of the sea.' " Soul and senses combine in passion to involve the totality of being in a disturbing experience, a synthesis of Platonic love and Epicurean pleasures.[23]

It is indeed this fusion of the whole being into a blissful state that constitutes what one may call privileged moments, which are rare and fleeting, for fickleness and the need for change are part of the human condition, as the poet knows from personal experience: "Shall ecstasy return that was, alas, my own? / Are lost delights that made life sweet forever gone, / Forsaking my soul in its dejected state?" ("The Two Doves," 210). The later fable is cast in lighter tone, as far as the doves are concerned, but the poet is quite melancholic in the concluding lyrical meditation. In *Adonis,* "poème héroïque," that is, a more stylized work, the tragic convention is operative: the hero's weakness brings on his death. The same vision, however, informs both works.

La Fontaine also deplores the diversion afforded by apparently useful activities. In hunting the wild boar that is laying waste to the countryside, Adonis seems to be undertaking a task of public usefulness: he takes the initiative, "assembles" his neighbors, puts himself at their head, goes into action, as in a later fable the judge and the hospital worker will do, desirous of serving their fellows. Their example permits the poet to declare in his concluding remarks:

> O ministers, judges, and you near the throne,
>   Who deal with the world of fact,
> You are the hampered whom misfortune has attacked,
> However powerful, whom good fortune corrupts.

Though you look at friends, it's as if your eyes were gone.
Then if there is a chance to think and be alone,
    Some flatterer interrupts.
("The Judge, The Hospitaler, and the Hermit" 12, 24,
                              p. 312)

By devoting himself to a community enterprise demanding physical
energy and courage, Adonis renounces self-knowledge, poetry perhaps, and activities of the mind that are essentially centered in the
individual conscience. Adonis, who "dreams at the sound of water,"
honored by the favors of Venus, goddess of love, could doubtless
be compared to his creator, a dreamer, a poet favored by the Muses,
who has learned to enjoy and celebrate the pleasures of love, as he
declares in the *avertissement* to the 1669 edition, by joining "to the
loves of the son, those of the mother" (*O.D.,* 4).

If the hero could not profit from his vanished love to make poetry
out of it, the poet uses the hunting episode to introduce an element
of diversity and contrast: after the idyll, we are offered a passage of
descriptive poetry, which might have aroused the interest of his
contemporaries, fond of that noble sport, leavened with humor. The
hunt gave La Fontaine the opportunity of introducing elements that
are essential in the *Fables:* animals, war, destruction, and death.
The interest of this episode has been well brought out: "Almost all
the heroism . . . seems to have come down from men to animals,
dogs, horses, boars, promoted to the dignity of heroic characters. . . . They already appear as the true heroes of the poem . . .
the serious and the tragic are tinged here with playfulness and
irony. . . . A parallel is drawn, to their advantage, which is a
prelude to the indictment, in the 'second collection,' of the alleged
superiority of man and the royalty he appropriates to himself over
the rest of creation."[24]

The adversary that Adonis and his companions confront is presented as the "tyrant of the forests." As such, it is the forerunner
of the lion in the fables, who, possessing strength, uses it as a
tyrant, dispensing arbitrary justice and practicing openly the most
brutal cruelty. The boar's depredations anticipate those of another,
less noble animal that will also provoke a fatal hunt. The complaints
of the farmers in *Adonis* announce those of the gardener in the fable
"Le Jardinier et son seigneur":

> L'avare laboureur se plaint à sa famille
> Que sa dent a détruit l'espoir de sa faucille:
> L'un craint pour ses vergers, l'autre pour ses
>   guérets;
> Il foule aux pieds les dons de Flore et de Cérès:
> ....
> Tâcher de le surprendre est tenter l'impossible.
>
>   (*O.D.*, 10)

> (Many a farmer complains to his family
> That its tooth has destroyed the hope of his scythe:
> One fears for his orchard, the other for his fields;
> It profanes the gifts of Flora and Ceres:
> ....
> To try to surprise it is to attempt the impossible.)

This situation prefigures, in noble style, that of the previously happy owner of a garden devastated by a hare, now at his wits' end:

> Our man informed the squire of the indignity.
> "This demon devours every seed I've sown," he said.
> "Morning, noon, and night, he laughs at any strategy
> The sticks and stones I hurl fall innocuously;
> He's a sorcerer."
>   "The Gardener and the Squire," 4, 4, p. 79)

Humor, already present in *Adonis,* becomes more evident in the fable. In both texts, hyperboles indicate distance on the part of the narrator, who appears somewhat detached, slightly ironic. In the fable, however, irony proves to be much more complex: the hare, so dreaded, represents like the boar, a natural destructive force, but it is minimal compared to that of the man. It is the squire, whose help has been solicited, who is gluttonous, dissolute, and brutal, and his men with "good strong teeth," who wreak havoc on the gardener, his crops, his daughter, and his kitchen garden. The evocation of the orchards and of the gifts of Flora recalls another fable in which a monster with a human face ruins the flowers and fruit cultivated with care and love, "L'Ecolier, le pédant et le maître d'un jardin":

> The schoolboy maimed the tree, did such harm in the end
>   That the fruit-grower, disheartened,
> Complained to the schoolmaster of the scapegrace,
> Who brought others until the orchard was overrun
>   By boys doing what the first had done
> Except that they were worse. . . .
>
> ("The Schoolboy, the Pedant, and the
> Man with a Garden," 9, 5, p. 213)

There always exists, with La Fontaine, in allegorical form or close to reality, a monster whose ignorance, stupidity, and brutality comes to destroy the balance and harmony of nature cultivated by humans who, through intelligence and labor, try to guarantee abundance and happiness. Adonis succeeded, at the cost of his life, in vanquishing the boar, a destructive monster. In the *Fables,* the monsters assume diverse forms, bestiality not being reserved for wild animals alone.

In *Adonis,* death strikes the hero when he is flushed with victory, at the moment when he triumphs over his foe: this noble end befits epic grandeur. Venus and Adonis, legendary figures whose story is offered as homage to a generous patron, were to know a fate commensurate with their status. The death of the hero, the grief of the goddess, are transfigured by the poet, desirous of creating a work in harmony with the grandiose setting of Vaux and furnishing his patron a refined pleasure. The poet had been able to observe at Vaux the creations of art allied with nature. He had known there a leisure that favored creative reverie and an awareness of his poetic faculties. From his secret conversations at this happy time with "the Nine Sisters" emerged his future artistic production.

The importance of *Adonis* is not limited to being an expression of the elegance and refinement in aesthetic matters of La Fontaine's patron Fouquet; nor is it limited to providing a preview of the themes that reappear in his best known work, the *Fables.* It possesses an interest and literary value in its own right. If the subject matter is a traditional one, suggested by La Fontaine's readings in Ovid's *Metamorphoses* and other works, its treatment is complex, original, and in the view of recent critics, thoroughly successful at the artistic level. La Fontaine manages the feat of uniting the idyllic, the heroic, and the elegiac. William Calin sees the poem as an illustration of "militia et amor." In his view, the tragic love story and the heroic deeds are placed in simple chronological succession by the author, without a real attempt at fusion. On the other hand, Jean-Pierre Collinet sees a clever concatenation; the heroic component, the hunt, placed in the middle of the work and culminating in the death of the hero, bridges the passage between the bucolic idyll and the elegiac lament. In our own study of *Adonis,* we have stressed love as the unifying element, the hunt as the departure and diversion from love being the tragic flaw that brings about the death of the hero.[25]

Adonis is a long, heroic poem of six hundred lines in alexandrine couplets: the verse form is as traditional as the subject matter. La Fontaine presents to his patron, later to the woman he loves, the traditional lyric themes: love, "omnia vincit amor"; the fugitive quality of youth and happiness, "tempus fugit"; sorrow and death. He uses topoi and poetic forms well established since antiquity. The literary conventions employed by La Fontaine—those taken from sources, and those used in setting, composition, and characters— have been carefully defined by Madeleine Defrenne.[26] The Adonis myth had been used by famous Renaissance poets Ronsard and Shakespeare.[27] Scholars have shown all that La Fontaine owed to the Latin poets, Ovid, Virgil, and Propertius, and through them to the Greeks, Theocritus and Bion, also to the Italian *Adone* by Marino.[28] But all the readings have been assimilated, reduced to poetic memories, to which La Fontaine added his own expressivity, thus providing for his readers "the twofold poetic pleasure of recognition and discovery."[29]

After having stated his admiration for the heroic style, La Fontaine confessed with charming ingenuousness in the *avertissement* that his poem was in fact rather an idyll, which is an accurate description of the first part of the text, that of the happy love story in the bucolic setting of the mountains of classical Greece. An idyll, in the etymological sense of the term, is a small picture, that is a relatively short poem, presenting a love theme in a country setting. But one finds in *Adonis* a counterpoint to the idyll in the tragic ending of the love story. The death of the hero and the sorrow of his lover bring about the use of another poetic style, the elegiac, typically dedicated since antiquity to the sufferings of unrequited love or to the loss of a loved one. As for the form, the elegy was not made up of stanzas, but had a distinctive meter, the elegiac distich. The themes and the form had been adopted by French poets during the Renaissance and the early seventeenth century: Ronsard

placed his *Adonis* in a collection of *Elégies;* Théophile de Viau, the
great baroque poet, also wrote *Elégies.*[30]

The second version of *Adonis* is even more polished in its diction
than the original one, as a stylistic study has shown.[31] Most important for us, the new dedication to Aminte, to whom La Fontaine
speaks as a respectful admirer, presents an offering of love to a
beautiful but as yet unyielding lady. There is therefore an underlying, unexpressed, but suggestive series of counterpoints between
the love story of the poem and the unfulfilled dream of the poet
who is cast in the traditional part of the unrequited lover. In contrast,
he is presenting to his lady-love an enticing picture of a fully realized,
idyllic love, hoping to convince her of the joys of such simple,
natural feelings. There is therefore in the second version a more
complex, more personal intention, which brings about a new sub-
tlety in the structure, the unrequited love of the poet framing[32] the
happily fulfilled love of Venus and Adonis, intended to persuade
the elusive Aminte of the sincerity of her lover.

The framing device is no doubt reinforced by the correspondence,
detected by a perceptive critic, between the two sets of characters,
the legendary ones and the personae of the poet and Aminte.[33] She
possesses the beauty, the graciousness, and the winning charm of
Venus; Adonis, like the poet, is a dreamer, carried in turn by joyful
enthusiasm and by melancholy, two major aspects of La Fontaine's
affectivity. Young Adonis lives a happy, carefree life in the peaceful
countryside, dear to La Fontaine, in the innocence of the Golden
Age, his only feat, like Hippolytus, being the hunting of wild
animals. He has not known love before his encounter with Venus
but gives in to it, most naturally.

In the same way, the poet has been taken by Aminte's beauty.
His attitude towards her is the traditional one of courtly love, which
remained a powerful model and ideal in seventeenth-century literature, seen in the novel and the theatre as well as in poetry.[34] He
presents to her the best of himself, his literary creation. The conventions of elegiac poetry are used to describe the sufferings of the
unrequited lover, the sublime beauty and charm of the lady, raised
to a divine rank in the opening invocation. The similarity between
her and Venus is thus emphasized. To entertain her, the poet is
going to recount the love of a goddess for a mortal, suggesting that
Aminte, like Venus, could well let herself be touched by a simple
mortal, the poet. The picture of shared love could possess a sugges-

tive power for her; the poem could have a spellbinding effect on Aminte. It is meant to hold up a mirror in which she will see such a seductive image of love that she will give up her defenses. In a subtle but provocative way, the poet invites his lady-love to explore the happiness of shared love.

In the poem, it is Venus who offers her love to Adonis. Of course, in the mythological world of gods and goddesses, social conventions do not apply. Love generates complete equality, without distinctions of rank and condition; a goddess can love a mortal without the least shame: " 'Tout est né pour aimer.' Ainsi parle Vénus." (*O.D.*, 7; "Everybody is born to love." Thus spoke Venus). This Epicurean position stressing the limitless power of love leads to a sensuous picture of the first moments of happiness of the lovers.

Equality and liberty create the perfect conditions for an ideal relationship. The lovers are temporarily projected in a world of their own, seemingly free from the constraints of time and death. But Adonis remains subject to his human condition and Venus herself, although immortal, has duties to perform: she has to satisfy her worshipers, to sustain her own cult. One can detect a sense of humor, a tongue-in-cheek assimilation of Venus to a high-ranking official who must attend to her public functions.[35] But the tone remains formal as the goddess invokes her duties, even Fate: "Il faut que je vous quitte, et le sort m'y contraint; / Il le faut. . . ." (*O.D.*, 9; I must leave you, Fate forces me to do so . . .). This creates a tragic situation: a separation of the lovers dictated by outside forces, duty and destiny. Such was the case for Dido and Aeneas, Titus and Berenice, the variant here being that it is the woman who is called away by a higher duty. But, as Venus entreats Adonis to take care of himself and stay faithful to her, she remains feminine, pathetic, and touching.

Tragedy follows, with the death of one of the lovers and the outpouring of sorrow that constitutes the elegy. The poet already knows how to move from one mode of diction to another; his virtuosity is even more evident in the *Fables*.

The passage from idyll to tragedy brings about a transmutation of all the elements that created the happiness of the lovers: the peaceful, intimate setting becomes a frightening wilderness, the warm presence of Venus a shadowy memory, the past bliss a vanished dream. The laments of Adonis foreshadow those of Venus at the end of the poem: both suffer in turn the pain of being abandoned by the loved one. This is, of course, a major theme in the elegiac tradition. Catullus had celebrated the sad fate of Ariadne; Ovid that of many abandoned women in his *Heroides;* Virgil that of Dido. This tradition remained very much alive in the seventeenth century not only in poetry but also in the theatre and the novel[36] with a new importance given to the man's sufferings, which the laments of Adonis would seem to illustrate.

When Adonis seeks a diversion in hunting, it suggests that he accepts the view of his peers, thus showing the weakness of the human condition, which, according to Pascal, needs diversion.[37] But Adonis does act as the leader of the young men living in the area and persuade them to fight the wild boar that destroys their properties, described as the "tyrant of the woods." He is thus implicitly compared to Agamemnon leading the flower of Greece against Troy and is thereby given heroic stature. His death will appear all the more glorious in an undertaking meant to guarantee peace and prosperity to his people. In the *Fables* La Fontaine uses epic, heroic diction for both tragic and comic effects.

The hunt episode, quite long, was considered "the weak part of the poem" by Paul Valéry who nevertheless saw some humorous features in the sketches of the hunters.[38] Seventeenth-century readers probably appreciated this description of their favorite sport. For the poet it may have seemed desirable to balance the two lyric sections, the idyll at the beginning and the elegy at the end, with a middle section devoted to heroic action. Whatever reasons inspired La Fontaine, the elaborate and lengthy description of the hunt has perhaps a jarring effect on modern readers, breaking the mood created by the lovers' separation.

This mood is reestablished by Adonis's death: he dies as a hero and a devoted lover. His last words and thoughts are for his beloved who mourns her loss pitifully but in vain: "L'Enfer ne lui rend point le bien qu'elle a perdu. . . . (*O.D.*, 18; Hades does not give back to her the lost beloved . . .). Sorrow and despair are depicted through physical details that are just the reverse of the ones mentioned at the beginning: the hair floating sensuously in the breeze becomes bedraggled; the glittering eyes, full of tears.

Venus's invocation to her dead lover brings back the theme of abandoning love for other pursuits: Venus had left Adonis to accomplish her duties as goddess, while Adonis had sought to forget the pain caused by her departure in the excitement of the hunt.

The implicit lesson is clear. Love alone can provide lasting happiness and contentment. La Fontaine already suggests one of the major themes of his later works: in *Psyché,* and in the *Fables,* he again sings of the simple but unique bliss of a shared life. And in his last book, the example of Philémon et Baucis brings the theme to a full and final orchestration:

> Ni l'or ni la grandeur ne nous rendent heureux;
> ....
> Hyménée et l'Amour, par des désirs constants,
> Avaient uni leurs coeurs dès leur plus doux
> Printemps.
> Ni le temps ni l'hymen n'éteignirent leur flamme. . . .
>   "Philémon et Baucis," 12, 25)

> Neither wealth nor high rank make us happy.
> ....
> Hymen and Love, through lasting desires
> Had united their hearts from their earliest age.
> Neither time nor marriage smothered the flame of their love. . . .)

In *Adonis,* the poet has to follow the main lines of the legend and adopt the tragic ending, with the poignant leave-taking of the bereaved Venus: "Je ne te verrai plus; adieu cher Adonis!" (*O.D.,* 19; I shall never see you again; adieu, dear Adonis!). This prefigures Racine's famous line: "Adieu, Seigneur, régnez: je ne vous verrai plus." (*Bérénice,* 5.7.1494). As a matter of fact, Valéry very aptly emphasizes the kinship between the two poets.[39]

Venus's invocation to Fate brings up the paradox of the powerlessness of a divine being who is thus brought down to a human level where she can inspire pity, one of the Aristotelian tragic emotions. The supremacy of love over any other human pursuit, clearly suggested, makes of *Adonis* an hymn to love in which both its happy and tragic aspects contribute to the beauty of the poem. The formal aspect is striking: La Fontaine uses in his poetic closure the majestic diction of the hymn, in the invocation to the divinities of the underworld, to the various *loci amoeni* where Venus and Adonis had known happiness. Nature does take part in the sorrow of the bereaved Venus: the poem ends on a cosmic note.

In his first masterpiece, La Fontaine realizes an idealized, platonic vision of beauty, of fleeting human happiness, and of love and death.

He could have placed as an epigraph *Et in Arcadia ego:* like Poussin, the great classical French painter, he recaptured and revitalized the elegiac tradition, aware of the two fundamental dramas of human existence, thwarted love and death.[40] The aesthetic principles of La Fontaine and of French classicism are already implicit here, that of abstraction and idealization of very real and universal human feelings.

During that same period, 1659–61, La Fontaine worked for his patron on a composition destined to celebrate the beauty and grandeur of Fouquet's country estate, Vaux. Because of the arrest and trial of the surintendant, the poem remained unfinished. It was a command performance and obviously La Fontaine's heart was not quite in it. The very concept was a laborious one since Vaux was in the process of being built and barely finished at the time the poet worked on this project. But La Fontaine found an ingenious way to get out of this difficult assignment, on which he spent almost three years, according to his preface to the work (*O.D.,* 78). It was to project his description into the future through the well-established device of the dream, hence *Le Songe de Vaux.* Fragments of this ambitious project were completed at the time of Fouquet's arrest on 5 September 1661. Four of them were published during La Fontaine's lifetime, the other five after his death in the 1729 edition of his *Oeuvres diverses.* The order of the fragments adopted by modern editors is that of the 1729 edition, but there is no proof that it was the order intended by the author. In the introduction to her edition of *Le Songe de Vaux,* Eleanor Titcomb proposes a different order, based on the statements in the *avertissement* of 1671 and on the text itself. She suggests that the fragments fit a chronological pattern based on two days and one night, starting with the visit to the château, a walk in the gardens, the night spent outside, and during the next day, the meeting with Aminte and the debate between the four fairies.[41]

In the *avertissement* preceding the three fragments published in the 1671 edition of his *Fables nouvelles,* La Fontaine explains his preference for the device of the dream, which had been consecrated by works as famous as the thirteenth-century *Roman de la rose* (1240–80), Francesco Colonna's Renaissance work, translated in French in 1546, *Le Songe de Poliphile,* and the classical "Dream of Scipio" in Cicero's *De republica.* He is also using another well-known device, the *débat* or contest between allegorical figures. Since he is dealing with a château and its park, the personified arts involved are Architecture, Painting, Landscape Gardening, and Poetry, each one arguing for the preeminence of her art. But he did not want to present to his patron and his readers too technical, too didactic a piece; he wished to please and entertain them. Therefore he planned to mix with the more serious parts episodes of a lighter nature: he mentions three of those, the adventure of a squirrel, which is no longer extant, that of a swan about to die, and that of a salmon and a sturgeon. His interest in the use of animal characters can be seen here. The choice of a squirrel was probably a reference to the presence of that animal in Fouquet's coat of arms, with the proud motto *Quo non ascendam?*,[42] an allegorical rendering of the minister's fast rise to the top. The other animals, the salmon and the sturgeon, fish living in water, were used to evoke the canals, fountains, and reflecting pools of Vaux: the park's beauty was enhanced by water, as Versailles was to be. It was a sign of abundance and luxury, displayed for the pleasure of the viewers.

In the first chapter, the narrator, Acante, having fallen asleep on a spring night, visits the palace of the god of sleep, Morpheus. La Fontaine again used an episode from Ovid's *Metamorphoses,* which had been the major source for *Adonis.* Again, the setting is bucolic; the god's palace is located in the woods, protected against too much light and noise. Acante sees the god reclining on a bed of poppies and requests that the personified Dreams guide him through the wonders of Vaux.

The debate among the Sister Arts that constitutes the second fragment may have been inspired, according to Eleanor Titcomb, by the contemporaneous interest in the fine arts, illustrated by the founding of the Académie royale de peinture et de sculpture in 1648, by the translation into French of Italian treatises on painting, the *Promenades de Richelieu ou les vertus chrétiennes* by Desmarets de Saint-Sorlin in 1653, and the descriptions of Vaux by the art historian Félibien and Mademoiselle de Scudéry, the novelist.[43] The fragment is introduced by a dedication to a friend of Acante, Ariste, who was probably Pellisson; it was composed much later than the piece itself since the poet alludes in it to Fouquet's misfortune.

The debate takes place in the "Salon des Muses" at Vaux; behind a railing, on a dais are seats for the "demigods" and the judges. On the other side of the railing, the four contenders are seated. Palatiane, the Architecture fairy speaks first in anger against Apellanire, the fairy of painting. Her main argument is that she provides

shelter for paintings and her art applies to the planning of gardens
as well. Rome and the whole universe testify in her favor. Her
speech is proud, but she appears to make a favorable impression.

Apellanire answers her rival's argument, claiming that her art,
painting, gives pleasure:

> Car il ne s'agit pas d'être le plus utile;
> C'est assez de causer le plaisir seulement. . . .
>
> (O.D., 87)

> (It is not a question of being the most useful;
> It is enough to provide pleasure. . . .)

Her powers are of those of a magician: she can create the illusion
of life with colors on a flat surface, represent sad and tragic events
to delight the viewers, and give to a lover the consolation of possessing the beloved in a portrait.

Hortésie, the fairy of landscape gardening, charms the judges by
her unaffected beauty and modesty. She starts her speech by a disclaimer that is in fact a *captatio benevolentiae:* she does not know the
art of eloquence. It is obvious that La Fontaine knew the rhetorical
tradition learned in his "collège" days and going back to Cicero and
Quintilian since he applied its principles in the formal speeches of
the four fairies.[44] Hortésie's takes the shape of a Malherbian ode,
stanzas of ten octosyllabic lines with echoes of Virgil and Horace:
gardens and their waters[45] provide peace of mind and relaxation in
attractive surroundings to emperors, kings, and statesmen. She seems
very persuasive. But her rival Apellanire shows to the judges her
portrait in winter to remind them of the fragility of the charms
with which they were so taken, thus following the example of Roman
lawyers who showed to the judges pictures of the crimes suffered
by their clients.

The ode that constitutes the first part of the speech by Calliopée,
the fairy of poetry, follows again a Malherbian pattern with stanzas
of six heptasyllabic lines; its theme is inspired by one of Horace's
famous odes: poetry insures immortality to the event and the people
it celebrates.[46] This topos from antiquity was used by Renaissance
poets and by Malherbe whom La Fontaine admired greatly. Even
though Calliopée does not use marble, she nevertheless builds temples and, as in painting, creates illusions:

> La Peinture après tout n'a droit que sur les corps,
> Il n'appartient qu'à moi de montrer les ressorts
> Qui font mouvoir une âme, et la rendent visible. . . .
>
>   *(O.D., 94).*

> (Painting after all takes hold of the bodies alone,
> I alone can show the inner springs
> Which move a soul and make it visible. . . .)

Bucolic charms are more appealing in poems than in nature and poetry can paint and describe as well or better than painting. The Aristotelian doctrine of *imitatio* and the Horatian motto: *ut pictura poesis* are obviously referred to here, but La Fontaine through Calliopée does not hesitate to claim the superiority of their art: using nonmaterial signs, words, it comes closer to the essence of things.[47]

The third fragment, "The Adventures of a Salmon and a Sturgeon," recalls the *galant* style of Voiture: it is written in a light vein, opposed to the more formal, rhetorical style of the preceding debate. Since it deals with fish, the famous letter of Voiture from "La Carpe au Brochet" ("The Carp to the Pike") comes to mind. La Fontaine clearly intended to bring to Oronte, the poetic name given to Fouquet, and his wife, "l'adorable Sylvie," homage from all parts of the universe, here from the seas, through two ocean fish.

The following fragment offers another sample of *galant* style. La Fontaine uses the doctrine of metempsychosis in a humorous fashion. Titcomb believes that his source again was Ovid's *Metamorphoses* (15. 1, 60 et seq.) in which Pythagoras presents his ideas.[48] The fragment is written in lines of various meters, called "vers libres" (free verse), which the poet used extensively in the *Fables*.

Sylvie, Madame Fouquet, wishes to hear the song of a swan that is about to die and compare it with that of a famous musician, Lambert. The latter handily wins the contest. The poet consults the Pythagorean philosopher Lycidas, who claims that Vaux in its entirety, including the dying swan, is under the protection of Apollo who will become its overseer. This constitutes another hyperbolic compliment to Vaux's master.

The Muses appear to Acante, the narrator, in the next episode of the dream. They intend to celebrate Oronte-Fouquet, especially the Tragic and Comic Muses, Melpomène and Thalie: Fouquet's taste for the theatre was well documented; he commissioned plays by Corneille and Molière. La Fontaine probably refers to both:

> Melpomène pour lui peint les vertus romaines;
> L'autre imite toujours les actions humaines. . . .
>
> (O.D., 105)

> (Melpomene paints for him Roman virtues;
> The other one always imitates human
>   actions. . . .)

The poet then gives a luscious description of Le Brun's famous painting of Night, which was on the ceiling of the small room located next to the "Salon des Muses."

Next, the narrator sees in his dream a dance of Venus, Cupid, and the Graces in the meadows of the village of Maincy, close to the park of Vaux. It takes place in the moonlight with the prettiest nymphs of the area, that is the prettiest ladies, Aminte and Sylvie. Their dance is accompanied not by fiddles but by Cupid's song. The poet uses a *précieux* conceit: the god of love is wounded in his turn:

> Le sort veut que j'aime,
> Moi qui fais aimer.
>
> (O.D., 107)

> (Fate makes me fall in love,
> I who inspire love.)

At dawn, the narrator continues his wanderings and discovers Aminte asleep on a bed of violets in a sensual posture of complete abandon, her breast half bared, very suggestive to an admirer suffering from unrequited love. He is tempted to kiss her but foresees her anger and stops in time. The beloved wakes up and wants to flee. In this episode La Fontaine reworks the well-known topos of the sleeping beauty contemplated by a lover, found in novels, in *l'Astrée* by Honoré d'Urfé, which he knew very well, among others, and in poetry. He uses it again in his *Psyché* and *Clymène*. The mixture of prose and verse in *Le Songe de Vaux* also definitely foreshadows *Psyché*. Aminte, however, in true *précieux* fashion refuses to be touched by love.

In fragment 8, Neptune takes care to adorn the grotto with fantastic animals, probably suggested by *Le Songe de Poliphile*. La

Fontaine's artistry in this description has recently been compared to Madeleine de Scudéry's description of Vaux, basically factual, written in a reporter style. La Fontaine's more general, less specific account is considered more literary.[49]

The last fragment, "Les Amours de Mars et de Vénus," was inspired by a sumptuous piece of interior decoration, a series of eight tapestries representing the story of Vulcan. The literary sources of the episode are Homer's *Odyssey* (8, 266–366), again Ovid's *Metamorphoses* (4, 171–89), and his *Ars amatoria* (2, 561–600). The topic is an extramarital love affair among the pagan gods: it would therefore be fitting for La Fontaine's *Contes*, traditional lascivious tales but retold with humor and elegance. Here, however, the poet chose a strophic form, which is not the case for the *Contes*. The humor shows in the quick capitulation of Venus to the war god. Apollo had similar designs on her and in a fit of jealousy revealed the love affair to the deceived husband, Vulcan, who, in anger, drops his hammer and decides to avenge himself. The revenge motif is used here in a heroic-comic style. Vulcan, instead of avenging himself as a tragic hero, goes to Jupiter to complain about his misfortune, thus becoming a comic character, the traditionally ridiculous deceived husband. Jupiter, an adulterous lover, mocks him. Vulcan forges a steel net to catch his wayward wife and her lover *in flagrante delicto*, with the other gods as witnesses.

In a short epilogue La Fontaine alludes to the unfinished state of his work, caused by the fall of his patron. The most striking feature of *Le Songe de Vaux* is the mixture of genres. In its unfinished state, it remains a juxtaposition; a fusion attempted again in *Psyché*, finds complete and successful realization in the *Fables*.

As in *Adonis*, there is a lyrical side to *Le Songe de Vaux*, with its dreamy, supernatural aspects; there are also encomiastic and descriptive elements. In the lyrical, personal parts, we find Nature, Morpheus, Night, and Aminte whose presence, invoked in the second version of *Adonis*, is already important here. In the encomiastic and descriptive parts, we find a poetic evocation of Vaux's wonders and the praise of their master. Finally the episode of "Les Amours de Mars et de Vénus" could be considered an elegant preview of the *Contes*. The use of animals points to the *Fables*, but the poetic transmutation remains to be discovered; the full and complete synthesis appears in the first volume of the *Fables* in 1668.[50]

The patronage of Fouquet and the atmosphere of Vaux were

certainly beneficial to the poet in more ways than one and made a
deep and lasting impression on him as an artist and as a sensitive
person. He wrote a letter to his lifelong friend Maucroix detailing
the sumptuous festivities offered by the surintendant to the king,
the queen mother, and the brother and sister-in-law of Louis XIV,
known as Monsieur and Madame. This text constitutes an important
document in several respects; from the point of view of the formation
of classical taste, it stresses Molière's contribution: the playwright
is seen as bringing back Terence's elegant, natural style:

> Et maintenant il ne faut
> pas
> Quitter la nature d'un pas.
> (O.D., 526)

> (From now on, we must adhere
> To Nature very closely.)

The poet knows how much those years in Fouquet's orbit had meant
for his own artistic development. He remained grateful and loyal
to him during his years of trial and tribulation, a courageous attitude
in view of the king and his minister, Colbert's determination to
strike down too powerful and too lavish a subject.

La Fontaine wrote and published anonymously, without place or
date of publication an "Elégie pour M.F.," probably in 1662.[51] It
appeared later with other works of the poet. It is a lovely elegy,
full of sympathy for the unfortunate minister, thrown from a high
position to the despair of a life in prison. The poet asks the Nymphs
of Vaux to intercede in order to obtain Louis XIV's pardon and
clemency. He recalls the magnanimous behavior of the young king's
grandfather, Henri IV, after the civil wars and concludes:

> Inspirez à Louis cette même douceur:
> La plus belle victoire est de vaincre son coeur.
> (O.D., 529)

> (Do inspire to Louis this same gentleness:
> The greatest victory is to overcome one's feelings.)

Another tribute to the fallen surintendant is the "Ode au Roi"

and a letter to Fouquet of 30 January 1663, in answer to the remarks
made by the prisoner in reaction to the ode. It places the composition
of the ode at the end of 1662 or early 63.[52] The ode is written in
strophic Malherbian style; it is a formal appeal once again to the
clemency of the all-powerful king:

> Moins ta grandeur a de limites,
> Plus ton courroux en doit avoir.
> (*O.D.*, 530)

> (The less limited your power is
> The more limited your wrath must be.)

The classical example of Caesar is presented by La Fontaine; that of
Augustus must have been present in the mind of seventeenth-century
readers who knew Montaigne and had seen Corneille's *Cinna.*

The letter to Fouquet is remarkable for the tone of respect and
praise given by the poet to the judgment of the prisoner who had
prepared himself the legal arguments for his defense. In it La Fontaine reiterates expressions of loyalty, devotion, and concern for the
life of his former patron.

His attachment appears again in a moving passage of the *Relation
d'un voyage de Paris en Limousin,* a work composed of letters addressed
to his wife in August and September 1663 when the poet accompanied his uncle by marriage, Jacques Jannart, on his trip to Limoges
where he had been sent into exile by royal order. Jannart had given
to Madame Fouquet legal advice for the defense of her husband. La
Fontaine may have decided to go with his uncle as a gesture of
family loyalty and affection.

These letters were, according to some scholars, inspired by the
Voyage de Chapelle et de Bachaumont, published in 1663.[53] They are,
like *Le Songe de Vaux,* a mixture of prose and verse, probably intended
for a group of friends in Château-Thierry and members of the former
Fouquet circle. They were not published during the poet's lifetime,
a fact that would seem to indicate their private nature. The first
four appeared in 1729 in the *Oeuvres diverses.*

Recent scholarship has revived interest in this short but delightful
work, not only for its sophisticated narrative techniques, which
foreshadow those used in later works, especially the *Contes* and the

Fables but also because it reveals La Fontaine's deep understanding of seventeenth-century France.[54]

In spite of a disclaimer to his wife; "Vous savez mon ignorance en matière d'architecture, et que je n'ai rien dit de Vaux que sur des mémoires" (*O.D.*, 552; You know my ignorance in architectural matters and that all I said about Vaux was based on documents), La Fontaine shows a strong feeling and intelligent appreciation for man-made as well as natural beauty: of the Renaissance châteaux, Amboise in particular, in a strikingly picturesque location on a high cliff overlooking the river, of the well-ordered, classical layout of Richelieu, adorned with antique statues and modern paintings, as well as of the beauty of the soft Loire valley landscape, justly named "the garden of France."

The multifaceted interests of the poet are evident: in geography, in local customs and specialties: the ash-rose cap worn by Limousin women, the quality of the butter, carps and melons eaten on the way; in French history: the ruins left by the recent civil war, the Fronde, the statue of Joan of Arc in Orléans, the greatness of Richelieu the statesman. Personal factors play a part in his account. In Blois, the memory of Monsieur, Gaston d'Orléans, brother of King Louis XIII, was probably meant as an homage to his widow, Marguerite de Lorraine, who was to become his next patroness in 1664. Personal feelings are the strongest when he recalls Fouquet's imprisonment in the château at Amboise, after his arrest in Nantes. La Fontaine asked to see his cell, and since the key to it was not available, he spent a good deal of time contemplating the door and meditating on the sad fate of his former patron.

In spite of this tragic note, the general tone of the work is light and humorous. The poet teases his wife on her taste for chivalric romances and suggests that history would be an improvement in her reading habits, provided she would not show off her learning. He pokes fun at himself for his ignorance, his need of sleep, and constant attention to pretty women, either in life or in art. He mentions his son at the end of the first letter, joking that he might bring back a maid from Limousin to play with him. It seems from those remarks that he was not lacking in familial concern and affection. These come out strongly in the account of his visit to a relative on his mother's side. He speaks warmly of that relative, an older man, still active, happily married to a young woman with a large brood of children.

One can find in the *Relation* subtle links with the later works: the jokes about country priests and monks, the sketch of an affected provincial countess who tells the story of the trials and tribulations of an attractive woman of Poitiers, la Barigny, who had two successive lovers, pave the way to the *Contes*. A verse passage could be considered as a proto-fable: the people of the Beauce region complain to Fate about their hilly terrain. The god decides that from then on the people will carry the hills on their backs, hence the abundance of hunchbacks, and that furthermore the remaining hills will be removed to Limousin. The people of the Beauce, like the frogs in the Fable "The Frogs Asked for a King," dissatisfied with their fate, complained about it and in consequence received a worse one. La Fontaine was already in 1663 on his way to his masterpieces.

Chapter Three
Les Contes, Clymène

It seems likely that the praise for Gaston d'Orléans in the *Voyage de Paris en Limousin* was intended for his widow, whose protection La Fontaine obtained in 1664. The dowager duchess of Orléans, the former Marguerite de Lorraine, known as Madame, held court at the Luxembourg palace in Paris. It was built for Marie de Médicis, widow of Henri IV, on the model of the Pitti palace in Florence, by the French architect Salomon de Brosses. Begun in 1612, it had lovely gardens, Rubens paintings, and tapestries. It was truly a royal residence that could appeal to La Fontaine's esthetic feelings. The dowager duchess was, however, devout and surrounded by churchmen. The atmosphere of the palace was rather dull and joyless but the poet's duties as a *gentilhomme* attached to the household were not onerous if not well endowed and left him plenty of leisure: these years were in fact very productive ones.

Before he started his service at the Luxembourg in July 1664, La Fontaine, after his return from Limousin, spent time in Château-Thierry where he became a member of the duchess of Bouillon's circle. The former Marie-Anne Mancini, niece of Cardinal Mazarin, felt the need of urbane, witty companions in her country seat. It has often been said that it was to entertain the duchess that La Fontaine wrote his *Contes*. This tradition goes back to an eighteenth-century man of letters, Fréron,[1] mostly known today through Voltaire's epigram denouncing him as a vicious gossipmonger. Another source, a contemporary one, Brienne, is quoted as having said "La Fontaine wrote some contes for M. Fouquet, in order to make a living."[2] It may very well be that Fouquet before his fall, Madame de Bouillon, and other society people encouraged La Fontaine's writing of racy tales.

Moreover, the poet's friends in Paris, men of letters such as Furetière, Pellisson, and Maucroix met regularly to discuss literary matters. Calling themselves "les Palatins" or "the Knights of the Round Table," they provided a sympathetic audience for the *Contes*.[3] The tales certainly were very much appreciated in their time, even by an academician, that is a member of the French Academy, like Chapelain. They fit in with the new fashion of *galanterie,* which replaced *préciosité* in the 1660s.[4]

But there may have been more practical and pressing reasons for La Fontaine to publish his *Contes:* they brought to the impoverished author money and success. Modern editors have stressed this aspect of the undertaking. With the fall of Fouquet, publishers and booksellers were in a difficult financial position, so that they had to resort to the trade of bestsellers, entertaining fare capable of attracting a large number of readers.[5] The *Contes* did reach an appreciative audience and earned for their author quite a reputation. The fact that this result was gratifying to him is documented by the publication of new volumes or new tales almost till the end of his life; at the time of his religious conversion in 1693, he was made by his confessor to repudiate them as immoral, a notion he had steadily refused to endorse before, always claiming they were funny stories, written in jest. Because of this situation, we will discuss the *Contes* of the various periods together, as a whole.

In modern times, their reputation has plummeted. Today's readers no longer find them objectionable because of their "immorality." Situations that could lend themselves to graphic descriptions are presented in discreetly veiled terms. La Fontaine proceeded by allusions and innuendoes, leaving physical details to the imagination of his audience. The *Contes* have suffered from comparison with the *Fables,* to be sure. The conventional nature of plots and characters leads to a repetitive pattern. The bawdy story, the sexual joke, the stereotypes of the unfaithful wife, the cuckold husband, the lecherous monk or nun appear as worn-out clichés. This reaction was expressed by Paul Valéry, a great admirer of La Fontaine the lyric poet: he regrets the time La Fontaine wasted on the *Contes,* their pseudofolksy tone, the facile quality of their versification, their boring libertine atmosphere, the opposite, in his view, of true poetic sensuality.[6]

In recent years, the new interest in the *Contes* started with the publication of modern editions by foremost La Fontaine scholars, Pierre Clarac, Georges Couton, Jean-Pierre Collinet and Nicole Ferrier, and a book-length study by an American scholar, John C. Lapp. In the introduction to his edition, Georges Couton argues that they represent an important event in literary history. They differ from the raw, comical, burlesque tales of the sixteenth century;

they differ also from the sophisticated and lascivious ones of the
eighteenth century, which spin accounts of seduction and depravity.
The vast culture of La Fontaine, his open mind and varied interests,
come through in this work. The artist conveys visual impressions,
creating pictures in words of familiar scenes. Moreover, they reveal
the poet's personality, his ideas and feelings, his views on human
nature and society, his ironic, detached wisdom, and his smiling
skepticism.[7]

On the formal side, Lapp argues that the *Contes* should be seen
as illustrating "the esthetics of negligence" and representing a successful artistic wager: "In the *Contes,* La Fontaine wagers he can
make the inappropriate appropriate, the unpalatable palatable. In
doing so, however, he strives, not merely to tell less crudely what
earlier writers had set down with uncompromising earthiness, but
rather to transform the scabrous, to make it a point of departure
for realms unknown. . . . It is this quality of the unexpected, the
unforeseen, that makes so many of the *Contes* inimitable masterpieces."[8] In his later book-length study, the same scholar defines
negligence as *"Irresponsibility*—The author denies that this work has
any special purpose, moral or otherwise, except pleasure. *Spontaneity*—He rejects all rules past or present, claiming to write without preparation or preconceived pattern. . . . *Consubstantiality*—
The writer assures us that he and his work are one."[9] The critic
stresses La Fontaine's originality in his treatment of well-known
sources, the Italian storytellers, Boccaccio and Ariosto. One of the
best examples of this creative imitation is "Les Oies de frère Philippe," a tale very much admired by a woman of taste, Madame de
Sévigné, especially for its subtle ending.[10] Collinet also thinks that
La Fontaine was very free in reworking his Italian sources. Like
Stendhal, he created an idealized, embellished image of Italy, a
perfect setting for amorous adventures. He dreamt, under warm and
sunny skies of a freer, more passionate life; his *Contes* are his *Chro-
niques italiennes.*[11]

Among the Italian sources, besides Boccaccio and Ariosto, Machiavelli provided the basis for "La Mandragore;" later, in the *Nouveaux Contes,* La Fontaine turned to Aretino.

The Gallic tradition is well represented with tales inspired by *Les
Cent Nouvelles nouvelles,* a fifteenth-century collection of short stories,
and by Bonaventure des Périers, Rabelais, and Marguerite de Na-
varre. One should also mention folklore. Around 1659–60, the

exact date is not documented, La Fontaine composed a farce with elements of song and ballet, *Les Rieurs du Beau-Richard,* which shows that he was familiar with the comic folktale tradition. The same story was used in one of the *Contes* in 1665, *Conte d'une chose arrivée à Château-Thierry.* It follows a traditional sketch: a rich, lewd merchant believes he can easily seduce a poor shoemaker's wife. The husband owes him money and he hopes to obtain her favors in exchange for the recognition of the debt. The crafty wife hides her husband, makes the would-be seducer tear up the note, and signals to her husband by coughing. The coughing signal is also used by Molière in the seduction scene of *Tartuffe* (4. 5). The merchant is routed away. Another conte, "Les Rémois," published in the third part of the *Contes,* in 1671, is also based on local lore and probably an elaborate variant on a traditional theme.

In the prologue, the author praises the merits of the capital city of his native province, Champagne. National and local pride are celebrated along with more sensual pleasures. It was in Reims cathedral that French kings were consecrated and crowned; Champagne, of course, was already famous for its wines; its pretty women were very much appreciated by the narrator. In the *Conte* proper, a painter, successful with women, both as a painter and as a lover, has a crafty wife, courted by two neighbors. She tells them that her husband has gone on a trip and invites them to dinner. The painter comes back unexpectedly, so she says. She makes the two men go in a hiding place where they have to witness the seduction of their own wives by the painter.

One can see through this sample that the themes are typical of the racy, bawdy, misogynistic, so-called "Gallic" tradition that in fact goes back to antiquity, to Greek literature with Anacreon, Herodotus, and Atheneus, and to Latin literature; La Fontaine used Petronius's *Satyricon* for "La Matrone d'Ephèse," as well as Italian and French sources. He acknowledged his debt to "Maître François," that is, Rabelais, and "Maître Clément," that is, Marot.[12] That tradition was never interrupted if one thinks of the medieval fabliaux and farces. At the very moment of the publication of the first volume of *Contes,* in 1665, Bussy-Rabutin's *L'Histoire amoureuse des Gaules* appeared and its author was arrested and put in the Bastille. The same year saw the short-lived stage performance of Molière's *Dom Juan.* These three works reflected a taste common to the freethinking segment of high society, of *la jeune cour,* young people at court.[13]

The first and perhaps most famous story in the first volume, "Joconde," was entitled in the 1664 edition, "Joconde ou l'infidélité des femmes," a very characteristic title, giving the keynote of the collection. The treatment, far from being moralistic, shows a great sense of humor and an indulgent if ironic view of human nature, since men are portrayed as being just as faithless as their wives.

Both Joconde's and King Astolfe's wives illustrate the view proposed in the original title. Although their husbands are unusually handsome and attractive, they seem to prefer coarse, ugly lovers, perhaps because they were made to marry their spouses and did not have any freedom of choice. This may simply be a humorous example of old topoi: *de gustibus non est disputandum* and the contrariness of human nature.

In a charming, if ironic scene of leave-taking, Joconde's wife reproaches him tenderly for his departure in answer to the king's call:

> Quoi, tu me quittes, disait-elle,
> As-tu bien l'âme assez cruelle,
> Pour préférer à ma constante amour,
> Les faveurs de la cour?
> . . . .
> Va cruel, va montrer ta beauté singulière,
> Je mourrai, je l'espère, avant la fin du jour.
> ("Joconde," *Contes, 52*)

> (What, you leave me, said she,
> Are you so cruel
> To prefer to my faithful love
> The favors of the court?
> . . . .
> Go away, cruel one, go and show off how handsome you are,
> I shall die, I hope, before the end of the day.)

After this scene, which recalls a similar one in *Adonis* and foreshadows that of "Les Deux Pigeons," Joconde, absentminded husband that he is, comes back for the bracelet and portrait that his wife had given him and he had forgotten. He finds her asleep in her bedroom with a coarse, unattractive valet. His first reaction is a violent one; however, he keeps his anger in check, thus avoiding a scandal. The narrator approves this wise attitude:

Tous deux dormaient: dans cet abord, Joconde
Voulut les envoyer dormir en l'autre monde.
Mais cependant il n'en fit rien
Et mon avis est qu'il fit bien.

("Joconde," *Contes,* 53)

(Both were asleep: at first sight, Joconde
Wanted to send them to sleep in the other world:
However he restrained himself
And in my opinion he did the right thing.)

A similar misfortune happens to the king: the queen has secret trysts with an ugly dwarf, as Joconde discovers. Both the king and Joconde decide to seek revenge: they will travel incognito and have amorous adventures of their own. The fruit of their experience is that their wives are no worse than many others. They might as well live peacefully with them. The wives, after their husbands' absence and the freedom they have enjoyed, are ready to settle down in domestic harmony. All is well that ends well, seems to imply the narrator.

"Joconde" was the subject of a literary dispute. The author of the *Dissertation sur la Joconde* argues for the superiority of La Fontaine's tale not only over a tale by the obscure Bouillon, which was closer perhaps to the original by Ariosto, but more importantly over their common model. The critic believes that by distancing himself from the absurd situation provided by Ariosto, La Fontaine was able to present a humorous treatment of the story and make his readers laugh. By portraying Joconde as a man of the world, not unduly affected by the faithlessness of his wife, he makes the protagonist's moderation and wisdom believable, thus observing the classical principle of verisimilitude. If he had presented Joconde as deeply wounded by his wife's betrayal, he would have created a tragic effect, the exact opposite of the reaction he wanted to produce. The author states that La Fontaine had adopted the good taste of Terence and Virgil, a great compliment on his part, very much in keeping with the new "classical" trend of the 1660s. La Fontaine himself in his letter to Maucroix of 22 August 1661, mentioned in the preceding chapter, praised Molière for "bringing back in France the good taste and style of Terence" (*O.D.,* 525). The author of the *Dissertation* concludes in no uncertain terms: "confessons que Monsieur de La Fontaine aiant conté plus plaisamment une chose très-plaisante, il

a mieux compris l'idée et le caractère de la narration."[14] (let us admit
that M. de la Fontaine, having told in a more pleasurable manner
a very funny story, he has better understood the concept and character of the narrative art.)

In his *préface* to the first part La Fontaine refutes most of the
objections raised against his *Contes:* it is not a licentious, immoral
book; he has simply borrowed the traditional stories and observed
the rules of the genre, which requires a jocular, humorous approach.
It would therefore be silly to take seriously the jokes concerning
the deceit of women. He is telling stories in jest and his *Contes* will
never deter people from marrying. If some of the stories seem pre-
posterous and unbelievable, one must remember that truth and
verisimilitude are not the aim of the storyteller, but the pleasure
of his listeners. These basic tenets are restated in the preface to the
second part, which shows they were foremost in the poet's mind:

[le] principal point, qui est d'attacher le lecteur, de le réjouir, d'attirer
malgré lui son attention, de lui plaire enfin. Car, comme l'on sait, le
secret de plaire ne consiste pas toujours en l'ajustement; ni même en la
régularité: il faut du piquant et de l'agréable, si l'on veut toucher. (*Contes,*
95)

(The main point . . . is to keep the reader's interest, to entertain him,
to attract his attention in spite of himself, in a word to satisfy him. For,
as one knows, the secret of pleasing does not always consist in artfulness,
nor even in the observation of the rules: it is necessary to use the unexpected
and the pleasurable if one wants to appeal to the readers' feelings.)

La Fontaine quotes the masters of the art, Marot and Voiture,
and stresses the freedom of creative writers who can attain beauty
in their own way, sometimes putting rules and precepts aside. This
point had been made earlier in the century by Guez de Balzac about
Corneille's *Cid.* In a letter of 1638 he remarked that the *Cid* was a
tremendous success, even though the playwright had not observed
the rules.

One of the longest and better known tales in the second part,
"La Fiancée du roi de Garbe," tells the adventures of a young
princess, Alaciel, whose name may have a humorous connotation—
a celestial name for a creature with a very earthy career—[15] who
starts on a long journey to be married to king Mamolin. After an
encounter with pirates, a rescue by a young admirer and various

adventures, eight in all, which illustrate the accommodating nature of the princess, she is reunited with the king, having passed "through eight different hands." The king, however, proclaims his complete satisfaction with his bride. Like Joconde and King Astolfe, he shows wisdom and tactfulness, and avoids asking too many questions. This attitude, as in "Joconde," is praised: the "accidents of the road" should be taken with equanimity. It is easy to detect the continuity of thought on the part of the narrator, under the variety of stories and sources.

In the second part, one finds a few tales dealing with lecherous monks and nuns: "Les Frères de Catalogne," "L'Ermite," and "Mazet de Lamporechio." This stereotype was traditional in medieval and Renaissance popular literature. But attitudes toward the church and its representatives had changed with the reforms established by the Council of Trent and the Counter-Reformation. Georges Couton remarks that "L'Ermite" presents not only a lecherous monk but an hypocrite and sees a connection with the quarrel over *Tartuffe*, Molière's play about a pious hypocrite who tries to seduce his benefactor's wife. The play was forbidden from 1664 to 1669. Critics wonder why La Fontaine courted trouble by using extensively this stereotype, under attack on the stage, in the *Nouveaux Contes*.[16]

In the third part, published in January 1671, one innovation is the introduction of magic and fantastic elements. In "La Coupe enchantée," the magic cup reveals the faithlessness of wives. Again, just as in "La Fiancée du roi de Garbe," the conclusion is that "ignorance is bliss." More magic appears in "Le petit chien qui secoue de l'argent et des pierreries," but despite extraordinary happenings worked out by the fairy, husband and wife end up deciding to be mutually tolerant and trusting.

Some critics have singled out in the third part "Le Faucon" and "La Courtisane amoureuse." In those tales, genuine feelings seem involved. In "The Hawk," a young man in love with an insensitive lady is ready to give up his last and most precious possession, the hawk of the title, for her sake. The lady, deeply touched by the sacrifice of the cherished bird, rewards her faithful lover. The courtesan's story illustrates the miraculous changes operated by true love: they are such that the young gentleman offers to marry the courtesan.[17]

At the end of the third part of the *Contes*, La Fontaine inserted a piece labeled "comédie," *Clymène*, probably written several years

before the publication of the volume. It was not intended for the
stage, as the poet himself indicates in a short notice preceding the
text. Pierre Clarac, in his edition of *Oeuvres diverses* includes it in
the section *Poèmes* rather than in *Théâtre*. The date of composition
has not been determined for certain. It is usually thought to be
1658 because of the allusion in line 10 to "les surintendants": there
were two surintendants at that date, Fouquet and Servien, until the
latter's death in 1659. The most telling evidence, in our opinion,
is an internal, textual one: *Clymène* recalls in a very definite fashion
fragment 7 of *Le Songe de Vaux,* as Clarac acknowledges (*O.D.,* 805).

The narrator, Acante, the same poetic name assumed by La Fontaine in *Le Songe,* is in love with Clymène who is afraid of love and
does not want to return Acante's devotion. The similarity of situation
and tone with the Acante of *Le Songe* pleading with the insensitive
Aminte is striking. The setting and characters in *Clymène,* however,
are borrowed from classical mythology. Apollo on Mount Parnassus
complains to the Muses that there is no longer any good love poetry,
perhaps because there is no longer any true love. Having noticed
Acante's feelings for Clymène, he requests the Muses to sing about
them in various forms: eclogue, ballad, ode, dramatic dialogue,
pathetic and lighthearted in turn.

Does this invitation represent an experiment at blurring the dis-
tinction among genres, forms, or types of literary expression? It
may well be that La Fontaine wanted to prove his virtuosity, using
various models in turn, Marot and Voiture for light poetry, Malherbe
for the heroic, Horace for the moderate style. The setting changes
to the Hippocrene spring; Acante appears in person and recounts
Cupid's offer the night before to show him Clymène asleep, lightly
clothed. One recognizes here the similar scene in *Le Songe de Vaux*
between Acante and Aminte. Through Cupid's intervention, he
obtains here some satisfaction.

Collinet sums up *Clymène* as a "poetic comedy leading to a narrative poem,"[18] thus acknowledging the hybrid character of the
piece. He also sees in it an *Ars poetica* of sorts, preceding Boileau's
and very different from it since La Fontaine does not express a
dogmatic point of view but a personal one: an aesthetic of diversity
is suggested as a replacement for the doctrine of separation of genres.
For us, *Clymène* constitutes a link between *Le Songe de Vaux* on one
hand, and *Psyché* and the *Elégies* on the other.

We noted in the second part of the *Contes* the introduction of the traditional type of lecherous monk or nun. *Les Nouveaux Contes* in 1674 was to give first place to stories involving unholy representatives of the church. Neither author nor publisher applied for a *privilège,* that is an official permission. The place of publication was given as Mons, the publisher's name as Gaspard Migeon, probably intended as a cover-up.[19] La Fontaine used as a source Aretino's *Ragionamenti,* so the subject matter of this collection is licentious, even if the terms used remain decent. One of the most famous *contes* in this vein is "Le Tableau," referring to an erotic painting, usually covered. It depicts a fight between two nuns for the sexual pleasure provided by a course, lusty valet: the situation recalls Joconde's wife's similar leanings, but here it is described in detail.

The Lieutenant Général de Police, the police commissioner in Paris, La Reynie, issued an order forbidding the sale of the *Nouveaux Contes* in April 1675. The famous actress, la Champmeslé, according to Furetière, took care of the private sale of the volume (*Contes,* 19). Georges Couton sees in this official censure an intervention from *le parti dévot,* a group of devout, militant Catholics, scandalized by the erotic behavior attributed to characters belonging to the church. The critic notes, however, the absence of documents showing that the police actively pursued the author or the publisher and suggests that it was simply a warning.[20]

This would explain why the later tales were not presented in collection form, but were published with other works, two in 1682 with the poem "Le Quinquina," five others in 1685 in the *Ouvrages de prose et de poésie.* The poet is supposed to have promised, when elected to the Académie française, not to write any more *contes.* Furetière, a longtime friend, excluded from the académie, labeled him a "watered down Aretino." Bussy-Rabutin defended La Fontaine; Bayle and Fontenelle placed him above the "Anciens" for his creation of a new genre: La Fontaine's work was thus providing fuel to the famous literary quarrel, "la querelle des Anciens et des Modernes" that was to last from the end of the seventeenth century to the beginning of the eighteenth.

The *Contes* have attracted the attention of modern scholars and critics. We have mentioned the work done by recent editors and the book-length study, *The Esthetics of Negligence.* To those one must add a very stimulating attempt to place the *Contes* and other works of La Fontaine, *Psyché* in particular, in the *galant* climate of the second half of the seventeenth century, explored in depth by Jean-

Michel Pelous. He sees the search for sensual and aesthetic pleasure as a sociocultural phenomenon, as a hedonistic view of love that replaced the *précieux* concept, inherited from the courtly and Neoplatonic tradition, which made service, submission, and constancy ideal values. With the new trend, the ethical value of constancy is opposed by the natural inclination for a variety of experiences. A correspondence between rejection of constancy at the psychological level and search for variety and diversity at the aesthetic level is thus established.

Another direction in recent scholarship has been to explore the role of the narrator and the narrative techniques used by La Fontaine in the *Contes*. John Lapp had stated that "La Fontaine manages frequently to assert the presence of the narrator." Jean-Pierre Collinet through a detailed and perceptive study of the prologues—the totally original contribution of the French author since they do not exist in the sources—reveals the personal and contemporary meaning of the *Contes* where the narrator speaks in his own name.[21] In several of them, he discusses his art and proclaims his taste for variety and freedom, principles that La Fontaine had also defended in his *Préfaces*. The prologue of "L'Ermite" recalls Molière's *Tartuffe*, that of "La Coupe enchantée," *L'Ecole des maris* and *L'Ecole des femmes*: the narrator makes fun of men obsessed with the fear of cuckoldry. The prologue of *"Belphégor,"* one of the later tales, becomes a dedicatory epistle to the famous actress la Champmeslé whose matchless talent received delicate praise from her friend and admirer. The author is moved to elegiac lines in regretting that his old age prevents him from being more than a friend to the charming and talented lady. Not only does La Fontaine speak in his own name in these captivating prologues, he also carries on in them a dialogue with his readers: he quotes their remarks, answers them, and builds up a comic skit. The critic concludes that they may very well be the best part of the *Contes*, an opinion his thoughtful and sensitive study helps to establish.

Madeleine Defrenne has analyzed the constitutive elements of the narrated trip and their application to the narrative sequence in "L'Oraison de Saint Julien." She detects a skillful alternation of fortunate and unfortunate adventures destined to trigger the emotions of the reader for the characters involved. Although La Fontaine follows closely his Boccaccian model, he introduces personal elements coming from his own experience. She also points out that the search for motivation is used as a narrative technique.[22]

A semiotic approach, using the theoretical principles of A.-J. Greimas, has been applied to five contes by Jane Merino-Morais in an attempt to show that La Fontaine was consciously applying the same techniques, time and time again, with slight variants.[23]

To conclude, La Fontaine's originality in the *Contes* is not to be found in the subject matter or the themes but in his handling of traditional and borrowed material, in his narrative and poetic treatment of that material, and in his style. His reworking of his models is very free; so is his versification. As John Lapp aptly put it: "Various poets before La Fontaine tried their hand at *vers libres:* Corneille and Molière with particular success. However, it can be said at the outset, and without reservation, that La Fontaine shows unrivalled mastery and inventiveness in the *vers libres* of the *Contes.*"[24] His triumph in this type of versification was to be achieved in the *Fables*.

Authorial interventions are frequent and add a great deal to the impression of immediacy and spontaneity. The narrator's comments, his taste for addressing the reader directly, help to create the illusion of a pleasant relationship between them, as in a natural, familiar conversation between *honnêtes gens,* sharing a funny story in a friendly spirit.

The language is well suited to the various characters, spiced up with familiar and old-fashioned expressions that give freshness and piquancy to the retelling. All social levels, many different professions are represented with their specific vocabulary, customs, and activities: the nobility, the clergy, town and country folks. La Fontaine succeeds in creating a world of fiction, of fantasy that gives the impression of being alive. The genre required a certain amount of caricature and jest: they are there, but never heavy-handed. A light comic touch, a delightful sense of humor, even some lyrical passages show that the poet is never absent from his narrative undertaking. It is his unmistakable presence and his art that give to the *Contes* their charm, recognized by contemporaries and recaptured by recent critics willing to look beyond the conventional to the personal elements.

Chapter Four
The First *Fables* (1668)

Most La Fontaine scholars agree about the poet's constant desire throughout his life to acquire a reputation and to please his audience. The *Contes* had brought him success, but it was among a small, sophisticated group of readers. He probably wanted to reach a larger public and to secure the protection of a generous patron. It is a well-known fact that many of the artists who had worked at Vaux to create beauty and grandeur for Fouquet's estate were later employed by Louis XIV who knew a good thing when he saw one: as a man of taste, he had been impressed by Fouquet's achievement and tried to emulate him on a larger, truly royal scale.[1]

It was even more important to please the royal court. Since the fall of Fouquet, since the king's pension list in 1662 (which omitted the name of La Fontaine), since the honors and benefits heaped on Molière, the poet could scarely escape the ambition to win recognition and protection from Louis XIV. . . . There is no doubting the success of his campaign in favor of the fables of 1668. They could not have been dedicated to the young prince without the king's permission. There may even be some truth in the anecdote which tells of La Fontaine going to court in person to present a copy of the book to the king and to receive a sum of money as a reward for his literary efforts.[2]

It may seem strange to a modern mind that La Fontaine was writing the *Fables* as a didactic but entertaining book for a young prince at the same time as he was publishing his *Contes*. To him, it was perfectly natural to adapt to his intended audience, not a sign of a divided self and even less of hypocrisy. He clearly expressed in his tale "Pâté d'anguille" what he felt was a basic human and artistic need, using the line as a refrain: "Diversité c'est ma devise" (Diversity is my motto).

The choice of a short, didactic genre was consonant with the undertaking to "please and instruct" a royal child. The gesture of dedicating fables to the dauphin had a precedent: Gilles Corrozet had dedicated his to the dauphin Henry in 1542.[3] La Fontaine "seems to have known Périgny, the prince's tutor, and he may have desired to win fame by preparing a book that could make some contribution to the prince's education."[4] A recent critic is convinced that La Fontaine's aim, as much as Bossuet's, but in a different style, was to educate French kings: the Grand Dauphin in 1668 and later the duc de Bourgogne to whom Book 12 will be dedicated in 1693.[5] There was a definite notion under the patronage of Richelieu and Louis XIV that men of letters and artists could contribute to the welfare of the state.

The fable, as a didactic genre, belonged to a continuous tradition going back to Greco-Roman antiquity. In the eighth century B.C., the Greek Hesiod included a fable in his didactic poem *Works and Days*. The best known Greek fabulist was the Phrygian Aesop, in the sixth century B.C. His fables are very short, straightforward prose texts that use mostly animal characters and end in a dry moral lesson. Aesopic fables were collected and reworked by Demetrius Phaleron in the fourth century B.C. and Babrius in the second century A.D. The Byzantine grammarian Planudes (1260–1330) produced a biography of Aesop and a collection of all known aesopic fables used as a source by later fable writers.

The major Latin fabulist was Phaedrus (30 B.C.–44 A.D.). He wrote elegant verse fables, imitated by later writers, Aphtonius and Avianus among others. The original text of Phaedrus's *Fables* was rediscovered in the Renaissance, in 1596; the first edition appeared in 1598 and a prose translation was done by the Jansenist scholar Le Maître de Sacy for students at Port-Royal.[6]

The enduring usefulness of aesopic fables is well documented. In the Middle Ages, collections of fables in Latin were used in the schools, and *ysopets* were written in the vernacular. The well-known woman writer, Marie de France, around 1180 composed the first *ysopet* in octosyllabic rhymed couplets in Old French: it contained 103 fables; she had many imitators.[7]

At about the same time appeared works of fiction in the vernacular with animals as major characters, written in octosyllabic rhymed couplets, grouped under the general title, *Le Roman de Renart,* Renart the fox being the central character. Animals, while keeping characteristic traits of their species, speak and act like people. The novels do not have the moralizing, didactic aims of the aesopic texts. In the works of the later cycle, there is some pointed social satire.

Modern scholars have seen *Le Roman de Renart* as an animal epic, parodying the famous Old French epic celebrating Charlemagne and other heroes. It is worth noting that elements of satire and parody appear in La Fontaine's *Fables.*

Both traditions were alive in the seventeenth century. The aesopic one was used in schools for didactic purposes: students were given a short fable as a basis for a rhetorical exercise of *amplificatio,* to develop their skills in the domain of eloquence. The native tradition was carried through oral transmission and appealed to aristocratic men and women, not familiar with Latin. A fusion of both was realized by La Fontaine in his *Fables.*

He had at his disposal at least three seventeenth-century compilations: those by Boissat, Audin, and Nevelet that had appeared between 1610 and 1644: "Nevelet's *Mythologica aesopica,* a collection of Greek and Latin fables ranging from Aesop to Abstemius, the Greek ones all accompanied by translations into Latin, was a rich storehouse of fable literature which may have proved very useful to La Fontaine."[8]

Moreover, various scholars became interested in the genre, Ménage and Patru among others. The latter included several fables in French prose in his *Lettres à Olinde* and recommended that writers use the greatest concision possible in constructing fables. Although Patru was a much respected lawyer and scholar, considered a master of judicial eloquence, La Fontaine did not heed his advice and preferred the poetic fable with the elaboration of an entertaining narrative and stylistic devices.[9]

To the Greek and Latin fables must be added the Indian ones by Pilpay (or Bidpai) translated into French in 1644 as *Le Livre des lumières ou la conduite des rois,* "a book which eventually became one of La Fontaine's sources of material,"[10] mostly for the 1678 collection.

In addition, as Georges Couton has demonstrated, he relied on emblem books, very popular since the Renaissance. The most famous was probably that by the humanist Alciatus, published in 1531. The "emblem" was composed of a title, an illustration, and Latin verses defining the subject matter, followed by a commentary. Because of the taste for allegory, authors of fables adopted the emblem format. Thus, Baudoin published in 1631 his *Fables d'Esope phrygien traduites et moralisées* with great success. La Fontaine was to use both formats, the short aesopic narrative, followed by a moral, and the emblematic one, complete in three parts, or simplified, as he saw fit.[11]

The importance of the illustrations in La Fontaine's *Fables* has been stressed. He was interested in all the arts, as can be seen in *Le Songe de Vaux* and his *Voyage de Paris en Limousin*. His disclaimer, stating he was not an expert, meant that he did not have technical knowledge, but he certainly showed a very sensitive appreciation. Following the custom of illustrated fable and emblem books, the publisher of the 1668 *Fables*, the Paris bookseller Barbin, secured the services of the fashionable engraver François Chauveau, who had done the frontispiece for the *Adonis* manuscript written in calligraphic hand by Jarry.[12]

The fable was considered a didactic genre, not a poetic one: it is listed in Aristotle's *Rhetoric*, not in his *Poetics*. Boileau did not include it in his *Art poétique* in 1674 nor did La Fontaine mention it in his presentation of the various poetic genres in *Clymène*.[13] He had therefore to create a new poetics for the kind of fable he was writing, the *fable ornée* or *fable égayée*, the fable as a developed and expanded poetic piece, capable of entertaining and charming the readers, besides presenting a useful lesson. To do so, he fortunately had at his disposal a storehouse of topoi, themes, and literary devices found in lyric and epic poetry and in romances ancient and modern. André Gide's famous remark that the *Fables* are a miracle of culture has been reexamined. Georges Couton does recognize that La Fontaine, while using the traditions, goes far beyond them in creating a new kind of fable and underlines the poet's pride in himself as a pioneer in the terrae incognitae of poetic invention.[14] La Fontaine himself asserted:

> J'ai fait parler le Loup et répondre l'Agneau.
> J'ai passé plus avant: les Arbres et les Plantes
> Sont devenus chez moi créatures parlantes,
> Qui ne prendrait ceci pour un enchantement?
> ("Contre ceux qui ont le goût difficile," 2, 1, *Fables*, 59).

> (Meanwhile, I've attempted what I think rather new,
> Had a wolf speak and lamb reply as never hitherto;
> Not merely this: my plants and trees are eloquent

As well as the animals you hear descant.
Now who is to say that it does not enchant?
(For those impossible to please, 2, 5, 35).

Jean-Pierre Collinet, while stressing also the difference between
La Fontaine's *Fables* and his aesopic models has attempted to define
what he drew from his readings: His knowledge of Greek appears
problematical; his Latin training was that of the average educated
man of his time—in Horace, Virgil, Terence, and mostly Ovid.[15]
But he knew extremely well all the contemporaneous literary production. He was steeped in *L'Astrée* and other lengthy romances of
the first half of the seventeenth century: Gomberville's *Polexandre*
and Madeleine de Scudéry's *Grand Cyrus* and *Clélie*. He confessed:
"Je me plais aux livres d'amour." (*O.D.*, 586; I enjoy love stories).
La Fontaine knew the works of Sorel and Tristan, Scarron, Furetière,
and Dassoucy. Among the poets, he shared views with the satiric
Régnier,[16] he admired the classical Malherbe and Racan, the baroque
Théophile and Saint-Amant, and the *précieux* Voiture.[17] He knew
how to conciliate and merge in his own poetry various trends, thus
realizing a fusion between classical order and harmony and baroque
fantasy and spontaneity.

The same can be said of his philosophical knowledge. He was
open to many new ideas while conversant with traditional systems,
the Epicurean one in particular. He knew Lucretius and the modern
interpreters of Epicurean thought, Gassendi and Bernier. He admired Descartes as an innovator, though he disputed his theory on
animals seen as mechanisms. He avoided dogmatic positions and
showed an inclination to freethinking. His libertine leanings, quite
obvious in the 1678 volume of the *Fables,* do not prevent him
however from expressing faith in Providence.

In his dedicatory epistle to the dauphin, La Fontaine hopes that
his book will both entertain and instruct the young prince whose
education is in excellent hands: the king made a happy choice in
selecting as a tutor for his son M. de Périgny.[18] His praise of the
king takes the conventional form of comparing him to Alexander
for his military feats and to Augustus for his wisdom as a ruler.[19]

The *préface* alludes to discussions held with a "master of French
eloquence," that is, Patru, about the distinctive characteristics of
the fable. Patru recommended that they be written in prose, with
the greatest concision possible. La Fontaine obviously did not share

his views: he claimed that the French did not appreciate a laconic style and invoked the public's judgment: his first fables had been well received, so he expected the same reaction to the collection (*Fables,* 5). His apologies for not having adopted the concise diction of his Latin models are quite disingenuous: he claims that he was not capable of emulating them but quotes an authoritative opinion [a classical authority, Quintilian], to justify his own choice for a fully developed and seductive form: "Quintilien dit qu'on ne saurait trop égayer les Narrations. . . . Je n'appelle pas gaieté ce qui excite le rire; mais un certain charme, un air agréable qu'on peut donner à toutes sortes de sujets, même les plus sérieux." (*Fables,* 7–8; Quintilian said a story cannot be too vivacious. . . . When I say humor I do not mean jocosity, but an alluring, irresistible something that can be imparted to any subject however serious.)

Ancient authority is called upon to testify to the usefulness and educative value of fables: Plato, while banishing Homer from his *Republic,* welcomed Aesop in it. The educative value is not only moral, but psychological: animals represent human character traits. As for the form, La Fontaine admits that he has not always followed the traditional pattern of dividing the apologue into body and soul, the fable proper and the moral precept, for aesthetic reasons.

In order to place his own *Fables* in the respected Aesopic tradition, La Fontaine felt that he should introduce his work by a *Life of Aesop, Phrygian,* inspired by the well-known but fictionalized biography by the medieval grammarian Planudes. Again, one sees the fabulist's desire to meet his readers' expectations while entertaining them.

The first volume of *Fables,* the actual books 1 to 6, was published by Barbin or Thierry in March 1668. Book 1 is preceded by a verse dedication to the dauphin, stating the author's purpose in mock-heroic style, with the traditional encomiastic prophecies on the glorious future of the young prince. The first line is a spoof of an epic beginning:

> Je chante les Héros dont Esope est le Père
> Troupe de qui l'Histoire, encor que mensongère,
> Contient des vérités qui servent de leçons.
> Tout parle en mon Ouvrage, et même les Poissons:
> Ce qu'ils disent s'adresse à tous tant que nous
>   sommes.
> Je me sers d'Animaux pour instruire les Hommes.
>   ("A Monseigneur le Dauphin," *Fables,* 31)

(I sing when Aesop's Wand animates my lyre.
Make-believe is here in its antique attire—
Insight confirmed by direct observation;
Even fish speak. As each find expression,
Animals enact my universal theme,
Educating men, fantasist though I seem.
"To His Royal Highness The Dauphin," 11)

Most commentators agree that it is probably best to examine each book in turn, since La Fontaine did not state his intention to establish an overall structure for the entire *Fables*. The first book, especially its opening and concluding selection, must have had a particular significance for the author: "As is true of most well-written beginnings, this first book of fables contains the structural elements of the whole and acts as a miniature model."[20] The first fable of book 1, "La Cigale et la fourmi" ("The Grasshopper and the Ant"), has been carefully examined, therefore, for clues to the design of the volume as a whole or to the thought or point of view that provided a focal element to the poet. At first sight, the narrative and the choice of characters seem to juxtapose two attitudes: the provident outlook of the hardworking ant who thinks ahead and saves for the bad days of winter, and the improvident one of the grasshopper who sang and entertained her listeners throughout the summer and is now starving. The fable is a short one, without a moral, written in light heptasyllabic verse, except for the even shorter second line, "Tout l'été" (All summer long). The summer has a double meaning: a carefree season of music and song for the grasshopper, a busy one of food gathering and preserving for the ant. This line, set apart from the rest, puts emphasis on the seasonal change and on time. In his thoughtful and sensitive analysis of the fable, Jacques-Henri Périvier has singled out time as the "essential reality."[21] He sees the opening fable as illustrating the double thrust of the whole Lafontainian oeuvre: the realistic and comic vision on one hand, the poetic and lyrical on the other. The major themes of the first are found in the greater number of fables and deal with the interplay of reality and illusion, presented in dynamic tension throughout the works. They derive from La Fontaine's acute observation of reality and lucid understanding of it. The poetic vision finds expression in the lyrical fables and in the poems, *Adonis* in particular; it is produced by the poet's secret aspirations to a better and more beautiful world, enhanced by love, dreams, and poetry.[22]

Traditionally, the fable was to show the dire consequences of improvidence and celebrate the merits of industry and careful planning. But in La Fontaine's fable, the ant appears as very cruel, totally lacking in charity, and to the modern mind typifying the worst traits of the bourgeois mentality. The economic aspect is underlined by the unsuccessful ploy used by the grasshopper who humorously swears "on her word of honor as an animal" to repay the ant, her prospective lender, before the following August: "Je vous paierai, lui dit-elle / Avant l'Oût, foi d'animal, / Intérêt et principal." ("La Cigale et la fourmi," 1, 1, *Fables,* 35). Some believe that the unsympathetic treatment of the ant, pitiless and sarcastic in her final retort, inviting the borrower to dance after having sung the summer away "—Vous chantiez? j'en suis fort aise. / Eh bien! dansez maintenant" means that the fabulist, implicitly, sides with the grasshopper-artist who sang for the pleasure of her listeners in a disinterested fashion, for art's sake. But "the ant has the last word," and no moral is expressed. What the author has presented is the way of the world: the greatest artists starve, although their creations live forever; wise and prudent people who know how to manage their resources live in comfort and, instead of extending a helping hand, mock the foolish ways of improvident, careless "neighbors." Even though the realistic world view seems to prevail at the fable's close, for Marcel Gutwirth, the lyrical element, present in the language, the rhythm, and musicality of the verse, is an implicit affirmation of the presence and value of the other view. The tension between the two remains in the poem as it does in life, the momentary triumph of the ant does not erase the permanence of the artist's creation.[23]

This underlying tension is seen as a model of equilibrium by David Lee Rubin: "To the narrator, even-handed judgment is necessary in this case. Both the grasshopper and the ant have qualities and defects that balance each other out, almost point by point. . . . The fable, therefore, presents an equilibrium where each embodiment of clashing attitudes appears partially validated but partially contradicted at the same time."[24] Thus the reader is implicitly invited to consider the opposite attitudes at the ethical and the aesthetic level where the ant can appear "as the embodiment of the *utile* and the grasshopper as a symbol of the *dulce:* though largely divergent and potentially antagonistic, each one without the other is insufficient and incomplete."[25]

The fables that follow, "Le Corbeau et le renard" ("The Fox and the Crow"), "La Grenouille qui veut se faire aussi grosse que le boeuf" ("The Frog That Would Be an Ox)," "Les Deux Mulets" ("The Two Mules") (book 1, 2, 3, 4), "La Besace" ("The Beggar's Wallet") "L'Hirondelle et les petits oiseaux" ("The Swallow and the Little Birds") (1, 7 and 8), introduce and develop another major theme of the volume, one that was often treated by the *moralistes* of the seventeenth century, that of *amour-propre* and *vanité,* self-satisfaction and blindness towards one's weaknesses and limitations.

"Le Loup et le chien" ("The Wolf and the Dog") has attracted very incisive comments from American critics interested in patterns of irony. The traditional reading sees this fable as an allegory of the superiority of freedom with deprivation over servitude with comfort. Recent criticism questions this interpretation, pointing out that, just as in the case of the ant and the grasshopper, there are good and bad aspects in both life-styles. The dog has a definite measure of freedom since he meets the wolf outside his master's property; he feels pride in the accomplishment of his task as a watchdog and contentment at the reward he gets: "Relatively little labor and ceremony (11. 23–25) are exchanged for material and psychological well-being. By contrast, the wolf is a wretch." He is also opinionated and biased. The dog, on the other hand, is pompous: La Fontaine keeps undercutting his characters: "Indeed, the only closure or sense of finality that the fable possesses is formal . . . the conflict between viewpoints never satisfactorily resolved."[26] It is probably the contrast between the two life-styles with their advantages and disadvantages that the poet intended to present to his readers. A similar line of argumentation appears in Richard Danner's perceptive analysis: "What is a perfectly natural course of action for the wolf might be disastrous for the dog. . . . Again and again La Fontaine stresses the importance of living in conformity with one's nature. . . . The dog never claims to desire freedom." No moral is stated; therefore a "multi-dimensional interpretation" is fully possible.[27]

According to Jules Brody, however, poetic discourse "should not mean but be. Its essential function is not message, but massage, not the communication of meaning, even multiple meaning, but the creation and manipulation of multiple attitudes towards meaning."[28] The critic sees a continuous, unraveling thread throughout the fable, made visible by the use of similar or related words: *peau-pelé, os.* The wolf is all skin and bone, the dog, sleek and well-fed, has a neck with a raw skin patch *(pelé)* and eats bones, "os de poulet, os de pigeons." Another thread in the text is the word *rien:* "the subjacent negative extension of the dog's courtly, affluent *embonpoint,* just as the chicken bones and the *col pelé* had announced the ironic transformation of the wolf's *maigreur.* Both these threads, moreover, lead in parallel fashion to the leveling of difference—physical, social rhetorical—between *le loup et le chien.* As a function of skin and bones and nothingness, one has become the other."[29] This interpretation, in spite of the previous disclaimer, leads back to a meaning, or a lesson: animal, and by extension human condition, is basically the same, whatever the superficial differences may be.

We have dwelt on these two fables in the first book because they have attracted the attention of recent commentators and are a good sample of the complexity and richness of these deceptively simple poems: far from being limited to children's instruction, they exercise the critical faculties of today's scholars.

Another example of reexamination of traditional interpretation is provided by Susan Tiefenbrun's reading of "L'Hirondelle et les petits oiseaux," usually seen as a lesson to the young to listen to the voice of experience. The critic shows that if the little birds did not listen to the swallow, in spite of her sound advice, it was perhaps because she did not practice a true art of teaching, she created distrust among her listeners by her negative attitude and her insistence on being different from them.[30]

"Le Rat de ville et le rat des champs" ("The Town Rat and the Country Rat") introduces in a delightful rhythmic form—the fable is written in short stanzas of heptasyllabic lines with an a b a b rhyme scheme—the traditional motif of the advantages of simple country life over the elaborate, luxurious city life. The theme has been used since Virgil and will reappear in Rousseau's writings and the romantics'. What makes it special is La Fontaine's humorous treatment of a conventional topos.

"Le Loup et l'agneau" ("The Wolf and the Lamb") is one of the most famous of all La Fontaine's *Fables.* Its lesson, hammered at the beginning, is one of the most cynical or ironical of the collection:

> La raison du plus forte est toujours la
> meilleure:
> Nous l'allons montrer tout à l'heure.
> ("Le Loup et l'agneau," 1, 10, *Fables,* 43)

> (Force has the best of any argument:
> Soon proved by the story which I present.
> "The Wolf and the Lamb," 1, 10, p. 21)

It illustrates the motto "might makes right." The wolf shows neither superiority of reasoning (all his arguments are disproved by the victim), nor any ethical consideration: he is hungry and has to eat. It is a matter of raw instinct and sheer physical power. "Meilleure" does not mean the best but the most efficient. The laws of the natural world, without any control or limitations imposed by civilization are given free rein. Nevertheless, even in such a primitive situation, it is noteworthy that the predator attempts to argue his case,[31] to convince his innocent victim of the justice of his destructive action. This is reminiscent of the pretexts invoked for wars of conquest. The theme of power has been considered by several critics as one of the major themes of the first *fables*. René Jasinski linked it with Fouquet's career and downfall, seeing the book as a reflection of a major contemporary political event that affected La Fontaine directly.[32] More recently, in his study of the iconography of the 1668 edition, Raymond Le Page states that the Chauveau illustrations stress the political meaning: this was understandable since it was meant for a prince who would, some day, rule his country: "What the illustrations reveal, above all, is the power theme. . . . In fact the whole book constitutes a survey of power relationships in the struggle for existence. . . . the major conceptualization of power that emerges in the original edition is that power must be exercised rather than merely possessed."[33]

"L'Homme et son image" ("The Man and His Reflection"), dedicated to La Rochefoucauld, author of the *Maximes,* published in 1665, picks up the theme of fable 7, "The Beggar's Wallet": self-love and illusions about oneself, also the main thread of the *Maximes.* In this fable the theme is presented through a mirror in which the man can observe his weaknesses. In the following fables, the poet comes back to political realities but in "Simonide préservé par les dieux" ("Simonides and the Gods") he deals with a topic that was very close to his own position: the condition of the poet in his relationship with his patron. There is probably an element of social satire in the fable: the patron, a Philistine, rewards the poet Simonides according to the amount of praise given to himself. The gods handsomely reward the poet who has praised them without expecting anything in return. This fable illustrates the concept of the poet's mission held since antiquity: Homeric hymns, the Psalms, Pindaric odes were written to praise, to enhance reality. Poets celebrating God or the gods, the reigning monarch, or beauty, should be given the rank that they deserve. With the help of an appreciative patron poets can find their place in the social order and their just reward, without starving like the grasshopper.[34]

Another very famous fable of book 1 is "La Mort et le bûcheron"[34] ("Death and the Woodman"). It can be seen as a meditation on the human condition, an evocation of the misery of the peasants in seventeenth-century France or an ironic view of human inconsequence. The woodsman, overcome by his misery, wishes to die:

> Il appelle la mort, elle vient sans tarder,
> Lui demande ce qu'il faut faire.
>   C'est, dit-il, afin de m'aider
> A recharger ce bois; tu ne tarderas guère.
>   ("La Mort et le bûcheron," 1, 16, *Fables,* 50)

> (So he called his mortal foe, and Death appeared
>   To ask why he had sent for her.
>   He said, "Just this; the wood I've cleared.
> Kindly cheer me by lifting the load I laid there.
>   "Death and the Woodman," 1, 16, p. 28)

The first book ends majestically with a fable considered to be one of La Fontaine's masterpieces and often anthologized, "Le Chêne et le roseau" ("The Oak and the Reed."). The symbolism is clear: the oak is the king of the forest, the reed represents fragility and flexibility. The presentation is very direct, without preamble or moral. The tragedy of the fall of the powerful and the survival of the weak, a traditional theme in Western thought and literature, found in the Psalms as well as in one of Sophocles' choruses in *Antigone,* receives a striking orchestration in this apparently simple, straightforward poem. The complexity, the richness of the language, the images, the rhythmic and phonic patterns have been analyzed with great care by commentators who have shown the supreme artistry of the poet.[35] One can detect a tragic irony in the oak's statement and an implicit compassion:

> Vous avez bien sujet d'accuser la Nature;
> ....
> La nature envers vous me semble bien injuste.
> ("Le Chêne et le roseau," 1, 22, *Fables*, 55)

(The oak said to the reed, "You grow too
unprotectedly. Nature has been unfair;
....
I perceive that you are grievously oppressed."
"The Oak and the Reed," 1, 22, p. 33)

It is the oak that becomes the victim of the force of Nature. The
periphrastic structures give amplitude and majesty to the natural
phenomenon, the storm,

> Le plus terrible des enfants
> Que le Nord eût porté jusques-là dans ses flancs

> (A fury of destruction
> Which the North had nursed in some haunt known to none),

and its terrifying effect, the uprooting of the tree, raised to the
mythic level of a giant:

Celui de qui la tête au Ciel était voisine,
Et dont les pieds touchaient à l'Empire des Morts.

(That thing of kingly height whose head had all but touched God's throne
Who had shot his root to the threshold of Death's door. p. 34)

The reversal is brutal, complete, overwhelming but sumptuously
and hauntingly described. No comments are necessary, the thun-
dering finale creates a lasting, cosmic, apocalyptic impression in
the reader.

   Book 2 starts with a fable presenting the poet's thought on his
art and his critics. We had seen the poet in allegorical form in book
1: the grasshopper, Simonides. This time La Fontaine uses the first
person pronoun and defends his choice of the fable as a genre: "Book
II of the *Fables* opens with a lyric as extraordinary in form as in the
problem it addresses. . . . to La Fontaine, the selection of a literary
genre is a function of temperament first and then of talent. . . .

The happy conjunction of both forces has resulted in his own great success."[36] In the fable La Fontaine makes fun of his critics in a parody of the epic: the subject is, as expected, the Trojan war and the conventional devices are used.[37] The result does not satisfy his critics who point to the lack of verisimilitude and suggest that the poet lacks talent for the high style. He tries a bucolic poem in a less exalted style. A critic is again dissatisfied, condemning the poet for a mere formal detail, a "rime pauvre," while the problem is, as David Lee Rubin notes, "a banal and insipid passage verging on the bathetic."[38] La Fontaine, in mock anger, answers him in short, rapid lines damning hypercritical, self-styled connoisseurs:

> —Maudit censeur, te tairas-tu?
> Ne saurais-je achever mon conte?
> C'est un dessein très dangereux
> Que d'entreprendre de te plaire.
> Les délicats sont malheureux;
> Rien ne saurait les satisfaire.
> ("Contre ceux qui ont le goût difficile," 2, 1,
> *Fables,* 60)

> (—"Harsh sir, pray spare your bearish mood
> Though a last word's something you'll not grant.
> No critical endeavor thrives
> Where one would try to suit your sort."
> The difficult lead fretful lives
> To please them, stop before you start.
> "For Those Impossible to Please," 2, 1, p. 36)

Although one could see these lines as a humorous outburst but inconclusive—"Though dramatic and closural, such a finale . . . leaves the impression that the issue has not been resolved in an intellectually satisfying manner"[39]—an important point has been made implicitly throughout the fable. La Fontaine, like Molière in *La Critique de l'école des femmes* (scène 6) rejects the traditional hierarchy of the genres and argues, as Molière did for comedy, that the humble fable requires as much talent as the epic or pastoral poetry.

The many ironies of "Le Lion et le moucheron" ("The Lion and the Gnat") have been perceptively analyzed by Richard Danner. The opening line, "Va-t-en, chétif insecte, excrément de la terre." ("Le

Lion et le moucheron," 2, 9, *Fables,* 67; "Begone, objectionable gnat, you pollute the air!" "The Lion and the gnat," 2, 9, p. 42), is a parody of a line by Malherbe attacking Concini, maréchal d'Ancre, hated minister of Marie de Médicis, executed on orders of Louis XIII. The contrast in size between the two animals is reversed in the length of their names, which are homophonic in their endings, thus creating a comic echo effect since they rhyme with each other. The critic remarks: "The ironist is aiming here in both directions at once: his barbs will strike the tiny winged creature as well as the haughty carnivore.[40] The mock-heroic style used to describe the war waged by the gnat against the lion, the futile attempts of the latter to defend himself are very funny indeed. Tragic irony appears in the final reversal:

> L'insecte du combat se retire avec gloire:
> Comme il sonna la charge, il sonne la victoire,
> Va partout l'annoncer, et rencontre en chemin
>   L'embuscade d'une araignée:
>   Il y rencontre aussi sa fin.
>   (2, 9, *Fables,* 68)

> (Mars' insect withdrew in a halo of fire.
> As he'd bugled the charge, he announced he'd retire—
> His last taunt to the tamed; then encountered a skein
> He'd not see, of a web which some spider had spread.
> He would never tame lions again.
>   2, 9, p. 43)

A relativistic view appears again in "Le Lièvre et les grenouilles" ("The Hare and the Frogs"): the hare who fears everything inspires fear among the frogs. It is clearly in evidence in the opening fable of book 3, "Le Meunier, son fils et l'âne" ("The Miller, His Son and the Ass,") thought to be one of the earliest fables and dedicated to La Fontaine's lifelong friend Maucroix, who might have hesitated in his choice of career, as Racan did in the prologue to the fable proper. The presentation is unusual, taking place at various levels: Maucroix's dilemma brings about the memory of a similar one in Racan's life, about which he consults his master, Malherbe, who tells him the aesopic story of the miller and his son going to the fair to sell their donkey; each of their moves has advantages and disadvantages, its partisans and its detractors. One should therefore do what one pleases and let people talk.

Another major theme evident in book 1 reappears in book 2, that of the laws of nature and their power. "La Chatte métamorphosée en femme" ("The Cat Changed to a Woman") shows that nothing, not even magic can alter the basic instincts given by nature. The man who was so crazy about his cat that he managed to have her changed into a woman and made her his wife is a fool:

> Il était plus fou que les fous.
> ....
> Maître sot en fait sa moitié.
> La voilà fou d'amour extrême,
> De fou qu'il était d'amitié.
> ("La Chatte métamorphosée en
> femme," 2, 18, *Fables,* 76)

> (A man one time become dementedly fond of his cat—
> ....
> Our Merlin wed her that very day
> And ecstatic folly reversed the gloom
> Of ill-starred love—sickness, I'd say.
> "The Cat Changed to
> a Woman," 2, 18, p. 51)

People should not trifle with the force of nature, which is infinitely more powerful and wiser than they.

The preoccupation with power and politics is taken up in book 3 by "Belly and Members" and "The Frogs Asked for a King." "Les Membres et l'estomac" seems to uphold the necessity of a hierarchy in the body politic, with the various members subordinated to one central organ.[41] However, as René Jasinski remarks, the praise of monarchy appears like a second thought, a duty that La Fontaine had neglected: it is only in book 3 that he takes up this important question. The critic also detects some irony in the comparison between monarchy and the digestive system.[42] Georges Couton sees in this fable an apologia for the personal government undertaken by Louis XIV. The function of the king is to uphold a stable social order, and in this regard, La Fontaine's position is very close to Pascal's conservative views.[43]

Discussions about various forms of government were traditional

among jurists and political philosophers since the Renaissance, culminating in the eighteenth century with Montesquieu and Rousseau.
Critics have linked "Les Grenouilles qui demandent un roi" with
political discussions on the merit of democracy and monarchy in
Corneille's well-known play, *Cinna,* and later in Bossuet's *Politique
tirée de l'écriture sainte.*[44] The frogs no longer want to live in a
democratic state, they go to Jupiter and ask for a king. He sends
them first a kindly king, a log. They complain to the god that their
king is too quiet. Jupiter then sends them a crane who gobbles
them up. In answer to their renewed complaints, he replies:

> Vous avez dû premièrement
> Garder votre Gouvernement,
> Mais, ne l'ayant pas fait, il vous devait suffire
> Que votre premier roi fût débonnaire et
>   doux;
> De celui-ci contentez-vous
> De peur d'en rencontrer un pire.
>   "Les Grenouilles qui demandent
>   un roi," 3, 4, *Fables,* 89

> (You should have managed to get on
> With the government of your own;
> But no. Your first king was one any frog could bear—
> Benign, gracious, in every way desirable.
>   Accept this one as suitable
>   Or endure a harsher with whom he can't compare.
>   "The Frogs Asked for
>   a King," 3, 4, pp. 61–62)

From these, critics have inferred that La Fontaine shares the views
of theoreticians and theologians of his time: they disapprove of
change for change's sake. Any system of government, being human,
has some weaknesses; the established one, to which a nation has
grown accustomed, becomes legitimate and is preferable for the
stability it offers. According to these critics, La Fontaine's point of
view is a conservative one at the political as well as at the social
level.

The political reality of raw force and sheer exercise of power seen
in "The Wolf and the Lamb" are presented in a more elaborate
fashion in "Les Loups et les brebis" (The Wolves and the Sheep")

and "Le Lion devenu vieux" ("The Lion Grown Old"): the wolves disregard the peace treaty made with the sheep since they are stronger; the subjects of the elderly and weak lion treat him with contempt since he can no longer defend himself.

Book 4 begins with "Le Lion amoureux" ("The Lion in Love"), dedicated to Mademoiselle de Sévigné, and takes the form of an epistle followed by the apologue proper, just as in "Le Meunier, son fils et l'âne," dedicated to Maucroix, the poet addressed his friend. Françoise de Sévigné was the beautiful daughter of a brilliant mother who had been, like La Fontaine, a loyal friend of Fouquet and who admired the poet. Before her marriage to the comte de Grignan, she had taken part in court ballets and shared her mother's social life in the Paris salons.[45] There was talk of the king's admiration for her, in spite of her reserve. La Fontaine's poetic homage was a courtly gesture to a fashionable young society woman:

> Celle-ci [la fable] prend bien l'assurance
> De venir à vois pieds s'offrir,
> Par zèle et par reconnaissance.
> ("Le Lion amoureux," 4, 1, *Fables,* 105)

> (This one, assured of your lenience,
> Attests its devotion embodied here,
> And kneels in sworn obedience.
> "The Lion in Love," 4, 1, p. 75)

Did the devotion and gratitude expressed here mean that the daughter, like her mother, had shown appreciation of La Fontaine's literary work?

Couton has speculated on the identity of the "lion amoureux" (*Fables,* 437, n. 2): was it the future husband, Grignan, or the king? Did La Fontaine in a humorous, allegorical fashion try to warn the young lady of the dangers attached to a king's attentions? It seems rather that the fable is an echo of "Le Lion devenu vieux" (3, 14): the king of the wilderness, deprived of his strength either by old age or by love is scorned and mistreated. The lesson of prudence applies not to the shepherdess but to the lion.

The form, remarks Jasinski, is quite literary, a verse epistle or a madrigal, written in isometric octosyllabic lines. Its tone is humorous, making fun of the fastidious taste of the *précieuses* while using their favorite style, the *style galant.* It became the model for the "society fable." Having completely transformed the genre, La Fontaine felt free to add variants according to circumstances. He also opened book 4 on a smiling, relaxed note. The illustrious name of the lady served as a protection against possible criticism from partisans of the aesopic fable; at any rate the moral, in spite of its lyrical tone, was there to reassure them:[46]

> Amour, amour, quand tu nous tiens
> On peut bien dire: Adieu prudence.
> ("Le Lion amoureux," 4, 1, *Fables,* 106)

> (Love, ah Love, when your slipknot's drawn,
> We can but say, "Farewell, good sense."
> "The Lion in Love," 4, 1, p. 76)

For us, there is a clever and ironic twist in this charming fable: Mademoiselle de Sévigné is presented in the introductory part as distrusting love and having played so far the part of "la belle in- sensible" (the beautiful cold woman). La Fontaine therefore presents to her a "fabulous" love story, since she cannot be touched by real love. But the love story developed in the fable proper proves that she is right: love has dangerous consequences for whomever lets him/ herself be carried away by his/her feelings. It is also dangerous to love someone belonging to a different species or class from one's own. Allegorically, it is unwise for a lion (a king) to love a shep- herdess (a charming young woman, but not of royal blood) and reciprocally for a shepherdess to love a lion, even if he promises to file his nails and teeth.

The same lesson of prudence is applied to a man possessed by another passion, greed, in the next fable, "Le Berger et la mer," ("The Shepherd and the Sea,"), illustrating the saying "A bird in hand is worth two in the bush." The poet comes back to the weakness of human nature in "La mouche et la Fourmi" ("The Fly and the Ant"), showing self-love and self-satisfaction. But the danger of association with the powerful is humorously illustrated in "Le Jar- dinier et son seigneur," ("The Gardener and the Squire,"), one of the most delightful fables of book 4, perhaps because it is an account of a contemporary happening. Both Couton and Jasinski note that the basic situation of a guardian who does more damage than the people he is to keep away exists in one of the aesopic collections, but no equivalent of La Fontaine's charming story has been found. The poet may well have witnessed such an occurrence in country life around Château-Thierry and used it as he did use local lore in the *Contes*. The happy and prosperous owner of a vegetable garden sees his crops damaged by a hare. He complains to the local squire who offers his help, comes with his hunting party, eats the farmer's provisions, attempts the seduction of his daughter, and destroys completely the prized garden. Most critics agree that one should not interpret this fable as a political denunciation of aristocratic privileges, that of hunting in particular. The peasant is presented as foolish: he should have known better and not have called his squire.

The theme of the deceiver deceived, present in the previous books, is illustrated here in "La Grenouille et le rat" ("The Frog and the Rat"). It has been well analyzed by Richard Danner[47] who points out the double meaning of "je vous ferai festin," "I shall treat you to a sumptuous meal" but also "I shall have a sumptuous meal out of you." The rat is obviously self-indulgent:

> Un rat plein d'embonpoint, gras, et des mieux nourris,
> Et qui ne connaissait l'Avent ni le Carême. . . .
> ("La Grenouille et le rat," 4, 11, *Fables,* 116–17)

> (A sleek round rat sunk in materiality,
> For whom Lent was not lean and Advent ever profane. . . .
> "The Frog and the Rat," 4, 11, p. 87)

He is easily persuaded to let himself be attached to the frog who sees a good meal in prospect: her perfidy as well as the foolishness of the rat are punished. The kite eats them both,

> Ayant de cette façon
> A souper chair et poisson
> (4, 11, *Fables,* 117)

> (Having caught for delectation
> Meat and fish in combination.
> 4, 11, p. 88)

The fable ends thus as it started, on a gastronomic feast, but of a different nature than the one planned: irony is not absent. An allegorical picture of social and political intercourse emerges, with treachery and greed ever present.

Danger is not absent either from domestic, family life: "Le Loup, la chèvre et le chevreau" ("The Wolf, the Goat and the Kid") shows the necessity of constant concern for one's safety; "Le Vieillard et ses enfants" ("The Old Man and His Sons") that of harmony and trust among brothers. On the other hand, "L'Oeil du maître" ("The Eye of the Master") and "L'Alouette et ses petits avec le maître d'un champ" ("The Lark's Brood and the Farmer") illustrate the positive side of self-interest.

Book 5 opens with a fable dedicated again to a friend and literary adviser of the poet. The initials M. L. C. D. B. have been interpreted in two ways by scholars. Recent editors of the *Fables*, Couton and Collinet agree with La Fontaine's biographer, Louis Roche, that those initials are those of le comte de Brienne[48] since the two men knew each other and collaborated on the *Recueil de poésies chrétiennes et diverses*, a Port-Royal undertaking. The Jansenists chose Brienne as editor, reserving the right to supervise his selections (*O.D.*, 939–46). La Fontaine contributed to this volume and wrote the dedication to the Prince de Conti.

In the first part of the fable, La Fontaine discusses literary matters: his friend's taste, which he shares, has guided him. Simplicity is best but does not exclude refinement. Similar views will be expressed by Boileau in his *Art poétique* in 1674.[49] The goals shared by the two poets, "plaire et instruire" (to entertain and to instruct), are those of the 1660 classical aesthetics. It is in this dedication that La Fontaine gives the celebrated definition of his work:

> faisant de cet ouvrage
> Une ample comédie à cent actes divers,
> Et dont la scène est l'Univers.
> Hommes, Dieux, Animaux, tout y fait quelque rôle:
> Jupiter comme un autre. . . .
> ("Le Bûcheron et Mercure," 5, 1, *Fables*, 134)

> (I have drama as it should,
> Expand to all-embracing theater,
> With scenes of every character;

> Men, gods, or animals, aiding me with a role—
> Even Jove himself. . . .
>> ("Mercury and the Woodman," 5, 1, p. 101)

The mention of Jove introduces his messenger, Mercury, whose name appears in the fable's title. The master of the gods remains the protagonist since the woodsman's prayer is addressed to him, and his judgment is final. Under the mythological names, one can detect here the concept of an omniscient as well as omnipotent Providence, which will reappear in "Jupiter et le métayer" ("Jupiter and his Tenant").

One of the most successful fables in this book in poetic terms is for us "La Vieille et les deux servantes" ("The Hag and her two Servants"). The mythological allusions create an aura of beauty and remoteness, in contrast with the realistic elements of the maids' daily life, with their chores and hardships.[50] Their plotting to get rid of the rooster that wakes up their mistress misfires: the old hag stays up all night for fear of missing the morning call. The final mythological allusion, emphasizing the downfall, brings the fable to an hyperbolic and ironic conclusion: "La Vieille, au lieu du Coq, les fit tomber par là / De Charybde en Scylla." ("La Vieille et les deux servantes," 5, 6, *Fables,* 139; Avoiding Charybdis, they had fled to the hag— / Had swerved from the whirlpool to the crag. 5, 6, p. 107).

The existence of opposite values within the same reality and the difficulty for most people to accept such ambivalence are illustrated in "Le Satyre et le passant" ("The Satyr and the Visitor"). As Danner has pointed out, "psychologically as well as physically the satyr dwells in the dark."[51] He "dismisses the passerby without giving him an opportunity to elaborate." The critic does not accept, with good reasons, the traditional interpretation that the satyr was rejecting hypocrisy or duplicity. He views the satyr's reaction as fear of the unknown, of trickery; he is incapable of distinguishing appearance from reality and is therefore ridiculous by rational standards. Voltaire was right when he declared: "Le satyre était un sot" ("The satyr was a fool"). It takes intelligence, reasoning, and tolerance to understand and accept two opposite effects produced by the same cause.

There are again reflexions on the fabulist art in the introduction to the double fable at the beginning of book 6: fables are fiction and depict a fantasy world; a plain moral will bore the reader and needs the narrative to be made palatable. At the same time fables must fulfill the double goal of providing pleasure and instruction:

> En ces sortes de feinte il faut instruire et plaire,
> Et conter pour conter me semble peu d'affaire.
> ("Le Pâtre et le Lion," 6, 1, *Fables,* 153)

> (For a tale should preach and please simultaneously,
> With the moral disguised by what takes us unaware;
> A tale for the tale's sake is too slight an affair.
> "The Shepherd and the Lion", 6, 1, p. 118)

Again, La Fontaine reminds his readers that brevity was considered the essence of the fable among the ancients but he has somewhat added to his models.

Mythological characters appear in "Phébus et Borée" ("Phoebus and Boreas"), one of the better known fables in book 6, linked to the human world as in "Mercury and the Woodman." The Sun and the Wind see in the Fall a traveler well wrapped in his coat. They make a wager: who will be the first to take the coat off the back of the prudent man. Boreas raises a terrible storm to no avail; Phoebus warms up the soaked rider and succeeds in making him take off his coat: "Plus fait douceur que violence. ("Phébus et Borée," 6, 3, *Fables,* 156; Clemency may be our best resource. 6, 3, p. 121).

The pride and arrogance of humans who think they know better than the gods is denounced in "Jupiter and His Tenant":

> Concluons que la Providence
> Sait ce qu'il nous faut, mieux que nous.
> ("Jupiter et le métayer," 6, 4, *Fables,* 157)

> (And so we see that Providence,
> Not we, should be our caretaker.
> 6, 4, p. 122)

The poet opposes to human limitations in matter of knowledge and judgment the wisdom of Providence. Jasinski points out the fusion between a mythological god and a Christian Providence.[52] This syncretism is typical of the seventeenth-century mentality, as several scholars have shown convincingly.[53]

"Le Cochet, le chat et le souriceau" ("Mousie, the Cat, and the Cockerel"; 6, 5) denounces the danger of judging on appearance and thus can be linked to "The Satyr and the Visitor," with a reversal: the satyr distrusted too much, the young mouse is too trusting.

The last fable, "La Jeune Veuve" ("The Young Widow"), is one of the most delightful of the collection. Some critics have suggested that rather than being a fable it is a *conte.* To be sure, La Fontaine was to make fun of a widow who is easily consoled in the *conte* "La Matrone d'Ephèse," published in 1682; but the circumstances and the tone are vastly different. The fable is infinitely superior, to our mind, in its delicacy and lightness of touch.

Richard Danner believes that La Fontaine has opted for irony in his treatment of the topos "time conquers grief." This intention appears in the first lines, with "excessive alliteration" of the plosives, the mourning summed up as a lot of noise and the contrast in the same line between noisy grief at first and subsequent resignation:

> La perte d'un époux ne va point sans soupirs.
> On fait beaucoup de bruit, et puis on se console.
> ("La Jeune Veuve," 6, 21, *Fables,* 170)

> (Of course when a husband dies who has been dear,
> One sighs brokenhearted sighs; then grows philosophical.
> 6, 21, p. 135)

The critic notes perceptively that "the imaginary flight of sadness on Time's wings is conveyed with anapestic swiftness." Thus readers are prepared to react to the young woman's plight from an ironic vantage point, "given our superior knowledge of the dynamics of grief."[54]

The humorous tone is maintained throughout: the husband's death is described by a periphrasis, "partait pour l'autre monde" (was leaving for the other world), the mourning of the young widow in terms that in a different context—tragic or elegiac—could be moving, but here seem exaggerated, creating a comic effect.

In contrast to these excesses, the father is presented as an "homme

prudent et sage" (a prudent and wise man): he provides the foil
against which his daughter's pronouncements appear all the more
fanciful and amusing: "Un Cloître est l'époux qu'il me faut.
("La Jeune Veuve," 6, 21, *Fables,* 171; "Ah, I'm wed to the veil since
he's gone." "The Young Widow," 6, 21, p. 136). Danner stresses
the absurdity of the idea "that a convent might literally, physically,
replace the widow's husband. . . . At the same time, the mention
of a convent marks a change in the widow's emotional state: she is
no longer asking to join her spouse in death."[55] The progression
from the wish to join her husband in death, to a convent, to a
return to normal life, then to thoughts of a second marriage is
skillfully built up. The initial image of flight, "Sur les ailes du
Temps la tristesse s'envole. . . ." 6, 21, *Fables,* 170; Sure to be
healed by Time, whose flight cures all. . . . 6, 21, p. 135), is
picked up at the end with the mention of other winged creatures,
Cupids or their human incarnations:[56]

> Tout la bande des Amours
> Revient au colombier. . . .
> (6, 21, *Fables,* 171)

> (Suitors were besieging her
> Once more the dovecote was thronged. . . .
> 6, 21, p. 136)

The lightness and gaiety of these lines marking the complete reversal
in the attitude of the young widow is remarkable and highly entertaining. Danner notes the sardonic tone of the expression "ce
défunt tant chéri" (this departed beloved).[57] The father does not
have to use any more persuasion, it is the daughter who takes the
initiative:

> Où donc est le jeune mari
> Que vous m'avez promis? dit-elle
> (6, 21, *Fables,* 171)

> ("Where is the marvel you promised, who soon will be marrying me
> Whom you said was incomparable?"
> 6, 21, p. 136)

As he does in the *Contes,* La Fontaine is using a model, here a fable by Abstemius, and elaborating on a topos, "time the healer." The antifeminist stance that can be read in "The Young Widow" belongs to a long literary tradition, expressed in medieval farces and fabliaux, and in satirical and comic works. It rests on the premise that men are endowed with the higher rational faculties while women are subject to their emotions and instincts. Such is the case with the young widow, carried by her emotions at first to the extreme of wishing to follow her husband in death, then rescued by her natural instincts. One could, of course, find similar examples among widowers. Couton points out that Abstemius had, in fact, told the story of such a widower (*Fables,* 463, n. 1 to "La Jeune Veuve"). The editor sees a satirical intent in La Fontaine's choice of the text involving a woman rather than a man. Collinet also states that, on the whole, La Fontaine paints a satirical portrait of women in the *Fables.*[58] In any case, "The Young Widow" is a delightful exemplum of the beneficial effects of time. One remembers that the volume opened with an example of the implacable effect of the seasons' cycle, in "The Grasshopper and the Ant." The reversal is complete and typical of La Fontaine's attitude: he recognizes and accepts ambivalence and paradox; his open and tolerant position is the opposite of that taken by the satyr, in "The Satyr and the Visitor." It is consonant with that of his model Aesop, who, according to the *Life of Aesop,* showed that the tongue could be the best and the worst thing in the world—a position that can be described as one of relativism.

The *epilogue* reaffirms La Fontaine's preference as a poet for a short and concise genre:[59]

> Bornons ici cette carrière.
> Les longs Ouvrages me font peur.
> Loin d'épuiser une matière,
> On n'en doit prendre que la fleur.
> (Epilogue, 6, *Fables,* 172)

(Our peregrination must end there.
One's skin creeps when poets persevere.
Don't press pith from core to perimeter;
Take the flower of the subject, the thing that is rare.
Epilogue, 6, p. 137)

In the epilogue the poet introduces his next work, *Les Amours de Psyché et de Cupidon,* for which the booksellers Barbin and Thierry obtained a *privilège* in May 1668 and which was published, together with the revised version of *Adonis,* in January 1669. The poet plays on the double meaning of "Amour": Cupid, Psyché's husband, one of the protagonists of the new work, and his love for a lady, which provides new inspiration (Georges Couton, *Fables,* 464, n. 4 to the epilogue). He also addresses a friend, Damon, who has urged him to work on *Psyché.* Who were the lady and Damon? The mystery remains in spite of the efforts of biographers and literary historians.[60] The important fact is that, in spite of this farewell, La Fontaine did not give up writing fables.

Chapter Five
Psyché

Les Amours de Psyché et de Cupidon must have been composed in at least two stages, one previous to the publication of the 1668 *Fables,* the other afterwards since La Fontaine stated in the *épilogue* of Book 6: "Retournons à Psyché. . . ." (Epilogue, 6, *Fables,* 172; Let Psyche be my theme again. Epilogue, 6, p. 137). It may have been started in the early 1660s since there are definite echoes of *Le Songe de Vaux* and a shared inspiration between the two works.[1]

The work is dedicated to the duchesse de Bouillon, the former Marie-Anne Mancini, niece of Mazarin, who had shown great interest in the *contes* and their author. She was a pretty, witty, fun-loving woman whose patronage was certainly important to La Fontaine. The same key terms used in the dedication of "Le Lion amoureux" to Mademoiselle de Sévigné reappear in the dedicatory epistle: "zèle et reconnaissance" (devotion and gratitude), addressed to the duchesse's powerful husband, who as lord of Château-Thierry had given his protection to the poet. The encomiastic themes are the expected ones: the duke's military exploits in the tradition of his glorious ancestors, especially his celebrated uncle, the maréchal de Turenne, one of the most famous military figures in seventeenth-century France, who is mentioned in the epistle. As for the duchess, the poet praises her "beautiful soul," her "quick wit," and her graciousness. In fact, she was "fort galante," that is she had many affairs, moved in a fast set, and at one point was sent to a convent: at that time it was the accepted way to dispose of women whose personal life had become an embarrassment to their husband and family.

The *préface* is important since La Fontaine speaks in it of the literary problems he encountered in writing the work, whose form is difficult to label. The author defines it as "une fable contée en prose." The term "fable" does not refer to the same literary entity as the *Fables* of 1668. It means a fanciful story, a fairy tale, a prose romance with mythological characters as well as contemporary ones. The second part of the definition, "contée en prose" (told in prose form), points to a narrative genre for the overall design, but it did not prevent the author from including poetic passages. The composition of the whole was however carefully worked out, as Renée Kohn has demonstrated, showing a well-balanced placement of the various episodes.[2] The fact that the composition was an elaborate one requiring protracted effort over a long period of time is mentioned by the author in the *préface*. There is a framing narrative, the "promenade à Versailles" of four friends who discuss aesthetic matters in a beautiful setting and listen to another narrative, the reading by Poliphile of his story dealing with Psyché's adventures. The reading is interrupted by discussions and descriptions of the Versailles gardens.

The main line of Poliphile's narrative, Psyché's adventures, came from Apuleius's *Golden Ass*.[3] But La Fontaine states in the *préface* that he attempted a fusion of the "galant," that is an elaborately amorous tone, with the fantastic and the heroic. His major goal was, as in all his other works, to please his audience, taking into consideration contemporary taste. He had learned from experience that it favored "le galant" and "la plaisanterie," that is the presentation of a love story in a light, entertaining vein: that is precisely what he strove to accomplish (*O.D.*, 123–24).

The author felt he was free to use his source as he saw fit, to make changes. He acknowledges the necessity of preparing the plot's resolution, without however destroying the suspense. His views are very much in agreement with those expressed by writers and theoreticians of the period. His basic principle, like theirs, is to bring together the useful and the pleasurable: this justifies his decision to insert poetic selections and to add the framing device. Thus it is difficult to identify *Psyché* as belonging to a specific genre. As Jean Rousset has suggested, it may deserve the definition Corneille gave to his comedy *L'Illusion comique*, "un étrange monstre,"[4] a strange, composite structure, using a variety of elements and styles, brought together by the art of the poet.

Although La Fontaine mentions only Apuleius, an ancient source, modern scholars have suggested others: Francesco Colonna's *Poliphili hypnerotomachia*, translated in French as *Le Songe de Poliphile*, Marino's *Adone*, canto 4 where the Psyché legend is mentioned, Benserade's *Ballet de Psyché ou de la puissance de l'amour* (1656), an episode of Tasso's *Jerusalem Delivered* (*O.D.*, 824) and d'Urfé's *Astrée*.

The setting used in the framing story, the Versailles gardens, imagined in their future beauty, as La Fontaine stated in the *préface*, recalls *Le Songe de Vaux,* so much so that Philip Wadsworth notes: "Indeed, the setting of *Psyché* is so similar in conception and style to *Le Songe de Vaux* that the novel can almost be called 'Le Songe de Versailles.' . . . Quite possibly La Fontaine began his version of the Psyché legend while under the protection of Fouquet, for he admitted that its composition was interrupted, without indicating for how long. But surely the 'encadrement' of the novel, if not the central plot, is the realization of an idea which was intended for *Le Songe de Vaux* and which the author could not bear to discard."[5]

The question of the identity of the four friends presented in the first sentences of *Psyché* has exercised the ingenuity of a number of scholars. The traditional attribution to the four major writers of the classical period, Racine, Boileau, Molière, and La Fontaine himself has been discarded after critical examination. Modern scholars tend to reject any specific equivalence with historical individuals.[6] The "promenade à Versailles" of the four friends is now seen for what it is, a literary device. The characters taking part in the outing and the literary discussion could very well be fictitious or allegorical. The figures may, as suggested by Jean Rousset, represent various literary genres[7]; Poliphile, the author of the Psyché story, having the task of harmonizing them. For Collinet, they represent different attitudes toward the passions.[8]

The freedom and informality of the conversation and discussions taking place among the four friends is remarkable. Poliphile, the narrator, wants the advice of his friends. At the request of Acante who loves gardens, flowers, and trees, an outing is arranged to an attractive country location. Poliphile shares his taste for natural beauty, but true to his name, loves everything. Thus, implicitly, he refuses to limit himself to one genre. The other two, Ariste and Gélaste represent through their temperament and taste tragedy and comedy (*O.D.,* 127–28). The link between *Psyché, Le Songe de Vaux,* and *Clymène,* all of which deal in part with the various arts and literary genres and their relative merits, is clearly apparent.

Another meaningful and telling association between *Le Songe de Vaux* and *Psyché* is established by the evocation and description of gardens, of a beautiful setting, bucolic and artistic at the same time: the art of the landscape architect Le Nôtre and the refined taste of the king have worked together to create with natural resources, a masterpiece.[9] Louis XIV's interest in natural history and appreciation of the beauty of exotic birds, animals, and plants gave birth

to the Ménagerie and the Orangerie, a striking conservatory where
orange trees and other rare species were grown. La Fontaine was
aware that Le Nôtre had planned the Vaux gardens and that the
orange trees of Versailles had been taken from Vaux (*O.D.*, 827,
n. 1). He must have felt pangs of nostalgia. Some may agree with
Pierre Clarac's remark that the setting is more attractive to the
modern reader than Psyché's adventures.[10] The description of the
Versailles gardens leads naturally to an encomiastic piece celebrating
the monarch who has so wisely chosen a hobby useful to his country:

Notre monarque se divertit à faire bâtir des palais: cela est digne d'un roi.
Il y a même une utilité générale; car, par ce moyen, les sujets peuvent
prendre part aux plaisirs du prince, et voir avec admiration ce qui n'est
pas fait pour eux. Tant de beaux jardins et de sompteux édifices sont la
gloire de leur pays. (*O.D.*, 129–30)

(Our monarch entertains himself by having palaces built: it is fitting for
a king. There is also in it a public usefulness. In this way, the subjects
can take part in the pleasures of the prince and admire what is not suitable
for them. So many beautiful gardens and sumptuous buildings contribute
to the reputation of their country.)

All this lavish praise was not rewarded. Did Louis XIV or his
minister Colbert find too much similarity between *Psyché* and what
La Fontaine had done for Fouquet? The response of the public was
not enthusiastic either. *Psyché* was in fact poorly received. Although
there was a counterfeit edition in 1669, no new edition came out
during La Fontaine's lifetime. Contemporary documents confirm
this lack of success, attributing misgivings to the publisher, Barbin,
who lost money in the undertaking.[11]
    After this introduction, the narrator mentions briefly a visit inside
the palace. He simply indicates that the four friends were struck
by the upholstery of the king's bedchamber, made of a Chinese
material with religious figures: one can glimpse here La Fontaine's
taste for the exotic, which will express itself fully in the second
collection of *Fables* in 1678. The party goes to the grotto of Thetys[12]
to find a cool spot. The water display is turned on for them. A
lengthy verse description of the grotto's ornamental features follows.
Louis XIV, the Sun King, is compared to the mythological Sun
coming to rest near the nymph Thetys at the end of the day. This
provides the perfect setting for the reading by Poliphile of his work.

Book 1 of *Psyché* follows the main line of the legend. It presents the characteristic features of a romance or a fairy tale: the extraordinary, superhuman beauty of the heroine, the jealousy of a powerful rival, the goddess Venus, and the latter's desire for revenge.[13] The tone and attitude adopted by the narrator towards the characters, however, change the nature of the story and the effect it produces on its readers.[14]

At the very beginning, for instance, Venus is turned into a very human person, as she was in *Adonis:* she fears a loss of her power (*O.D.*, 134). It seems absurd for a goddess to fear competition from a mere mortal. The inserted remarks about feminine nature recall the misogynist, satirical views found in the *Contes* and *Fables* (*O.D.*, 135–36). The skeptical, irreverent attitude of the narrator towards gods and heroes seems very modern: it undercuts the myth and its spell on readers, if it does amuse them. The narrator seeks their complicity when he states that the departure of Venus surrounded by Neptune's court requires poetry rather than prose (*O.D.*, 136). Gélaste, one of the four friends and the defender of comedy, makes a jocular remark: he would have preferred to see Venus depicted in a less formal fashion, in a grove, undressed as she was when she submitted to the judgment of a shepherd.[15]

These constant, recurring interruptions and humorous comments by the narrator or one of the members of his audience indicate that La Fontaine deliberately intended to undercut the mythological characters by disrupting the thread of the Psyché story and putting the reader on a kind of shuttle between the fantastic world of the legend and the fictional but contemporary world of the "promenade à Versailles" where Poliphile reads his work to his friends.[16]

Psyché, having lost her admirers because of Venus's wrath, is plunged into despair. So are her parents who consult an oracle. In true oracular fashion, the answer is that the husband chosen by the gods for their daughter is a "cruel monster who tears hearts apart," a veiled allusion to the god of love. The parents are to deliver her to her future husband by taking her to a mountain top in a funeral procession. Again the skepticism of the narrator comes to the surface when he remarks how superstitious the beliefs of those legendary times were (*O.D.*, 139). Psyché decides that she and her parents must obey the will of the gods, expressed through the oracle. The narrator, however, brings her decision back to a human, psychological level: she was simply desperate.

Abandoned at the top of a rocky, desert mountain in total solitude, except for some frightful, mythical beasts such as dragons and hydras, Psyché is flown by the Wind, Zéphire, to her intended husband's palace, illuminated as the upper spheres of the heavens where the gods dwell (*O.D.*, 142). Psyché is served by nymphs who, after a bath, dress her in rich bridal clothes, made by fairies "whose work usually cost nothing," another instance of the humorous treatment of the supernatural. The husband, after the wedding night, leaves without being seen. He asks his bride not to try to discover his identity nor to see him. Psyché is naturally consumed by curiosity. The husband she had not seen did not sound or feel like a monster, but in spite of this direct, experiential knowledge, superstitious beliefs overcome her common sense and reason: "si est-ce qu'au toucher et au son de voix il ne m'a semble nullement que ce fût un monstre. Toutefois les dieux ne sont pas menteurs; il faut que mon mari ait quelque défaut remarquable. . . ." (*O.D.*, 143–44; from the touch and the sound of his voice, he did not at all appear to me as a monster. However the gods do not lie; my husband must have some remarkably weak point. . . .) The next day, Psyché visits her husband's palace and is shown a series of tapestries. One of them represents Cupid on a chariot drawn by tigers. The power of the god is illustrated by four of the Olympians: Jupiter, Hercules, Mars, and Pluto being led by a small Cupid. In the sixth tapestry, Cupid bows in front of a beautiful young woman whose face is not shown. Love who conquers all is vanquished in his turn. It is, of course, a graphic representation of the protagonists, but Psyché fails to interpret the scene. But she is delighted to see portraits and statues of herself in various guises throughout the palace. A perceptive critic has recognized in this a manifestation of a self-love that will be replaced in the end by true love.[17] Spurred on by the paintings, Psyché tries on different costumes: this brings another comic interruption, by Acante this time, satirizing women's vanity and love of clothes (*O.D.*, 148).

After having enjoyed the gardens, Psyché ventures into the woods and happens one day to enter a grotto, cool and inviting. This is the topos of the *locus amoenus,* favorable to amorous pleasure and a replica, within the Psyché story, of the Thetys grotto of the framing device. One can see that the two levels are carefully built in echo fashion; a recent commentator describes it as a binary structure.[18]

In the darkest part of the grotto, Psyché meets her husband who complains that she does not know what true love is; if she did, she would seek solitude and silence. The rest of the story will show that in fact Psyché is immature and through trials and sufferings does learn to love in an altruistic fashion. Cupid's interdiction is reaffirmed, in spite of Psyché's attempts at discovering his secret. The god claims that if his wife had nothing more to wish for, she would become bored. If she discovered that he was a god, she would love him less, because gods are less passionately loved than human beings, another humorous touch (*O.D.,* 153–54).

The classical principle "to please and to instruct" is applied to Psyché's education. Through magic, she is shown events that will happen in the future: the Trojan war, the plays of the Greek tragedians. She is also taught "the secrets of poetry." The narrator makes fun of the conventional views on the corrupting influence of poetry and on the madness of the poet (*O.D.,* 155). These remarks about education tend to show that it is not in books that one learns, but through experience: the empirical, even the experimental point of view of La Fontaine shows through; he is close to Descartes,[19] very modern in his outlook. We pointed out earlier that Psyché should have trusted her experience and used deductive reasoning about her husband, which would have proven that he was not a monster.

In spite of her bouts of melancholy, Psyché is in fact quite happy. She should have realized that she was fortunate indeed and not asked for a greater happiness. She is like "The Frogs [Who] Asked for a King." The narrator, again in a misogynist remark, attributes Psyché's dissatisfaction and desire for change to her feminine nature, "incapable de demeurer en un même état" (156; incapable of remaining in the same condition). For Pascal, this weakness was part of human nature.

The jealous sisters put all kinds of doubts in her mind and provide her with a lamp and a dagger. Psyché hides her intentions under a show of affection, which brings another satirical comment from the narrator: she is acting the way all women do who are about to deceive their husbands (*O.D.,* 170). After some last minute hesitations, curiosity gets the better of her. She looks at her sleeping husband and recognizes with delight the god of love. A drop of burning oil falls on his thigh and wakes him up; retribution will come.

The reading of the Psyché story is interrupted, and the four

friends, having moved to another part of the gardens, start discussing
aesthetic matters. Psyché's situation is now quite pathetic: Acante
and Ariste are ready to enjoy the pleasure of shedding tears, but
Gélaste prefers an entertaining tale; since Poliphile started in a light,
humorous style, he should keep up in the same tone. The wise
Ariste prefers pity for its power on the readers but concludes: "il
est bon de s'accommoder à son sujet, mais il est encore meilleur de
s'accommoder à son génie. (*O.D.*, 175; It is a good thing to adapt
oneself to one's subject matter, but it is even better to adjust to
one's talent). La Fontaine had expressed this view in his fable "For
Those Impossible to Please."

A lively discussion about the hierarchy of genres follows. Gélaste
challenges the commonly accepted view that tragedy, triggering
pity and fear, is the noblest, highest one. We find here an echo of
Molière's views in his *Critique de l'école des femmes*. Gélaste argues
that comedy has become more popular than tragedy; the very terms
used to refer to theater and actors in general are "comedy" and
"comedians" (*O.D.*, 177–78). He brings up the traditional argument that laughter is the distinctive human trait. Ariste argues in
turn that tragedy offers a more refined, superior kind of pleasure.
The recent production of Racine's *Andromaque* is quoted by Gélaste
as an example of a tearful play, not likely to satisfy those who go
to the theater for entertainment. Ariste, however, believes that
tragedy can provide entertainment and pleasure through pity and
fear (*O.D.*, 180). After quoting examples from Homer and Plato,
Gélaste turns to reason, a typically seventeenth-century rationalist
and Cartesian attitude:

Mais laissons les autorités, et n'écoutons que la raison seule. Nous n'avons
qu'à examiner sans prévention la comédie et la tragédie. Il arrive assez
souvent que cette dernière ne nous touche point: car le bien ou le mal
d'autrui ne nous touche que par rapport à nous-mêmes. . . . (*O.D.*, 181)

(But let us leave aside the authorities and listen to reason alone. We can
simply examine without any preconceived notion comedy and tragedy. It
happens fairly often that the latter does not move us: because the happiness
or misfortune of others move us only as they relate to ourselves. . . .)

Ariste's reply is that pity is not sorrow; it is an altruistic emotion,
therefore elevating us to the sublime and making use of the sublime
style.

After this lengthy discussion, a verse passage brings the reader back to the beauty of the Versailles gardens and praises their creator, the landscape architect Le Nôtre, and the mastermind behind these wonders, the minister Colbert, Surintendant des Bâtiments since 1664, who supervises all the constructions. Colbert had been the archenemy of Fouquet and it was a rather delicate undertaking of La Fontaine to praise the person who had contributed to the fall of his former patron. Book 1 ends with a brilliant evocation of the 1668 festivities that took place in the gardens of Versailles, transformed into a fairyland (*O.D.*, 832, n. 62).

The second book is devoted to the wanderings of the unfortunate Psyché, abandoned by a wrathful husband determined to punish her. She is presented as guilty of a major transgression and thrown out of an edenic life into the outer darkness. The parallel with the Eve story is fairly obvious but the mythological names and setting give the author a way of escaping any accusation of irreverence.

Psyché finds herself alone, on top of a mountain, in the wilderness, as she was in book 1. She is tempted by suicide but the Wind, Zéphire, saves her. Cupid wishes to punish her, but he does not want her to die. The narrator, for comic relief, wonders why Zéphire did not fall in love with her (*O.D.*, 190). Obviously, Poliphile does not want his story to turn into a tragedy.

The location on a bluff overlooking a river and the thought of drowning must have reminded seventeenth-century readers of a similar situation in d'Urfé's pastoral romance, *L'Astrée:* rejected by the shepherdess (Astrée) he loves, Céladon attempts to drown himself in the river Lignon but is rescued by nymphs: an echo effect, if not an outright spoof, seems clearly intended.

Cupid declares to Psyché that he no longer considers her his wife but gives her as a slave to his mother, Venus, Psyché's jealous rival. At first, the unfortunate woman escapes the search made by her enemy and finds a shelter with an old fisherman and his granddaughters. She experiences the charm of a simple life and consults the old man who has chosen to leave the world and a high position to find peace in solitude. He tells her that, if she lets herself die, she will "destroy Heaven's creation" and show a lack of faith in Providence (*O.D.*, 200). He also gives Psyché hope for the return of her husband: his advice represents a Christian position, invoking the virtues of faith and hope. He also invites her to stay with his family in his simple abode in order to know herself and acquire wisdom: this lesson will reappear in the last fable, "Le Juge arbitre, l'hospitalier et le solitaire" (The Judge, the Hospitaler and the Hermit"). Thus, the old man's view proposes combining Christian virtues and the philosophical precepts of self-knowledge and wisdom in an ideal of peace and happiness, away from the passions and agitations that possess men and women living in the world.

Psyché replies that passions, love especially, are part of human nature and cannot be ignored. She questions the choice of a solitary abode for the two granddaughters, young women, eager to experience love. Thus to the philosophical point of view, she opposes the psychological one, to the mind and reason, feelings and instincts.

When she tells her story to the young women, two opposite reactions are voiced: the older advises submission to obtain her husband's forgiveness, the younger, on the contrary, declares that Psyché's curiosity was a proof of love, that her husband is unreasonable, and that she should let him come back to her (O.D., 209–10). Again, opposite attitudes are presented, each with its merits.

Psyché decides to look for her husband, to no avail. In desperation, she goes to one of Venus's temples to make her submission and obtain forgiveness, in the hope of seeing there Venus's son. In her wanderings, she passes the tombs of Megano and Myrtis, incarnations of beauty and grace. The superiority of grace over beauty is celebrated, as it was in *Adonis*.

Venus treats Psyché as a slave, has her whipped, and sends her on dangerous missions, hoping she will perish. But she is helped by one of Venus's maidens at the request of Cupid who seems more and more inclined to forgive his wife. Finally, Venus sends Psyché to Hades to get a box of Proserpina's make-up. Again an interdiction is uttered and a transgression takes place. Psyché must not open the box: one thinks here of the Pandora myth. Curiosity again makes her open the box, and her complexion becomes dark (O.D., 247–48). She has lost her last possession, her beauty, and takes refuge in a cave. Cupid finds his wife asleep at the entrance of the cave and kisses her hand. She flees inside, he follows her, throws himself at her feet, and admits his error and her innocence. She declares that she will always love him but does not hope that he will love her since she is no longer beautiful. They shed tears together; Poliphile, moved, drops his text and Gélaste, in jest, brings up the "pleasure of shedding tears" (252).

Cupid asks to see his wife. She replies laughingly that she could refuse to him what he refused to her in the past, but she will do whatever he wishes. Cupid asks Jupiter to give back to Psyché her true complexion and to place her among the deities of Olympus. A reconciliation with Venus follows, the happy couple produces an attractive daughter, Volupté.

A hymn to the new goddess, containing an allusion to the philosopher Epicurus, who claimed that pleasure is the mainspring of human actions, is well received by the listeners. Nevertheless, Ariste goes back to his original point: pity is the most pleasurable of emotions. It was when the listeners felt pity for Psyché that her story was most moving. Acante agrees but directs his friends' attention to the natural beauty of the sunset. The return trip takes place in the moonlight. Thus art and nature have joined forces during the day to provide a complete and refined enjoyment to the sensitive viewers and listeners.

Psyché, unappreciated in the seventeenth century and later overshadowed by the *Fables,* has attracted critical attention in the past decades. Its versatility appeals to modern taste, as well as the fact that it deals with the problem of poetics that is central to contemporary criticism, that of the relationship between the writer, the work, and the audience.

Psyché is composed of diverse elements. Jacques Barchilon distinguished "three elements, a description of the Versailles gardens, a *roman féerique,* and a Neo-Platonic dialogue," and pointed out La Fontaine's independence towards his sources. The poet refused to take seriously his mythological characters, viewed them with "ironic affection and amused tolerance," made a satirical use of literary conventions, *précieux* or pastoral, and through parody, created a light burlesque. But the "badinage" is never "overlabored," for "no one knew as well as La Fontaine how to convincingly mingle the comic and the poetic. This combination is the secret of the *Fables* and of *Psyché.*[20]

Other scholars have studied the rhetorical and technical aspects of the work. Margaret McGowan has shown how La Fontaine picked and chose in his sources, Apuleius's *Golden Ass* and Colonna's *Songe de Poliphile,* elements that he deemed essential to his story and the entertainment of his readers, leaving out the purely decorative or technical details.[21] John L. Logan has argued that preterition is "a key theme of the work as well as its dominant rhetorical figure." La Fontaine, through Cupid's remark to Psyché (*O.D.,* 153) indicated the paramount importance, on an aesthetic as well as on a psychological level, of leaving something unsaid. It has several advantages: it invites the readers to use their imagination, makes fun of literary conventions and of the narrative itself: "The parallels between Poliphile's language and both Cupidon's and Boileau's are remarkable: the importunate author bores his listeners; too much of anything is boring. . . . Cupidon's amorous secret is Poliphile's, and La Fontaine's poetic secret."[22] In his unpublished dissertation, the same critic has concluded that in *Psyché* La Fontaine reaches an "extreme degree of literary self-consciousness" and made "poetry out of literature."[23]

In a similar vein, Nathan Gross has noted how carefully La Fontaine avoided excess and has shown how cleverly he structured his work, the break between Part 1 and 2 allowing the transition from the comic to the tragic. The flaw in Psyché's character precipitates her sufferings, which lead her to self-knowledge as well as to pity for others' misfortunes. The frame characters also experience the tragic emotions so that "the digression strategically located at the center of the work functions structurally. . . . The whole frame functions strategically to place in clearer perspective our feelings before the spectacles of art and nature."[24]

The understanding of La Fontaine's aesthetics as expressed in *Psyché* owes a great deal to Jean Rousset's seminal and suggestive study, "*Psyché* ou le plaisir des larmes." The critic sees in the work a happy and harmonious combination of the poet's readings and of his dreams. Here, with the dialogues and exchanges between the narrator and his audience, the literary circuit is complete among author, work, and critic. The real protagonists are Poliphile the poet and his three friends who are invited to collaborate with him in the literary creation.

Comedy and tragedy can coexist and give pleasure placed, as they are in *Psyché,* in a skillful conjunction and harmonious balance. Ambivalence and reversal are illustrated throughout. At the end, it is Psyché who flees and does not want to be seen, and Cupid who pursues her. Her expiation has led her to know what true love is, as it has Cupid. The god of love has learned to love, having fallen in love with the soul of the beloved. Rousset recognizes the presence of a Platonic (later Christian) theme of the soul in quest of the divine.[25]

It is also in the Platonic aesthetic tradition that Jean Lafond places

Psyché. His study presents a full and illuminating discussion of the two concepts of beauty and grace, in seventeenth-century terms, the "je ne sais quoi." It shows that this new aesthetics is all the more significant in that it is shared: Méré, Bouhours, the author of the *préface* of the *Recueil de poésies chrétiennes et diverses*[26] argued, as La Fontaine did, for the superiority of grace and its freedom over beauty executed according to the rules.[27]

Specialists will consult with profit J-P. Collinet's detailed, exhaustive study of the genres and styles used by La Fontaine in *Psyché* in the context of theories of the time. The critic sees a basic paradox in the work: *Psyché,* which ends with the triumph of constancy is of baroque inspiration, in the evocation of the feelings as well as in its setting: La Fontaine wants to recapture in it "the natural language of the passions." Half way between Platonic idealism and Lucretian Epicureanism, *Psyché* owes its charm to this very ambiguity.[28]

Jacqueline Van Baelen presents an interesting transposition of *Psyché* into two dramatic structures, confirming the ambiguity of the work. The work as a whole can be seen as a five-act play observing the unities; the adventures of Psyché, as another play without the unities. The critic detects a third internal play, written and staged by Psyché for her sisters. The freedom of experimentation and creation is paralleled by the discovery of personal freedom: Psyché goes from ignorance and passivity to self-knowledge. Cupid, having married Psyché without her consent, made their union unequal and fragile. Happiness at the end is based on knowledge and free choice.[29]

There is a "disturbing darkness at the heart of *Psyché,*" according to Joan De Jean: La Fontaine warns his readers of the power and control the writer has over his public. The reader's curiosity "will never succeed in uncovering the secret of the works of art they are exploring, and thus obtaining mastery over them." Psyché's plight, caused by her curiosity, is also that of readers. It is the typical crime of intellectuals who want to know. Therefore *Psyché* "can be read as the story of an artist's desire for control over his public and of that public's frustrated curiosity." To gain control, the artist uses seduction, just as Louis XIV did at Versailles: he creates a brilliant machine, typical of classicism.[30]

A similar interest in the acts of reading, writing, and interpretation of text has led Michael Vincent to show the opposition between the presentation of the work and its basic theme. The presentation stresses "the essential orality of the work": Poliphile affects a "negligent style," the central digression is presented in the form of a dialogue; but, in fact "writing and reading necessarily impose themselves as theme."[31]

Noémi Hepp, using Rousset and Lafond's studies as a point of departure, traces a spiritual itinerary from eros to agape, from self-love to true, altruistic love. Through her ordeals, the heroine accomplishes an upward journey. To the act of transgression at the end of the first part corresponds an act of sacrifice at the end of the second part, since Psyché is ready to renounce her claims on her husband: this meaningful symmetry does not exist in the source. By lifting the weight of human selfishness, Psyché becomes a heavenly creature with wings. At the time La Fontaine was writing *Psyché*, in 1665–67, he was also translating poetic quotations in the *City of God* for Louis Giry's translation of Saint Augustine's famous work and working as one of the editors of the *Recueil de poésies chrétiennes et diverses*. Although *Psyché* cannot be considered a work of spirituality, threads of spiritual thought from Plato to d'Urfé and the Christian tradition are present in this fanciful, imaginative, and enchanting work.[32]

From the preceding analyses, *Psyché* appears as the triumph of art and a full expression of its author's aesthetics. It can also be viewed as a representation of the reader's curiosity being kept in suspense by an author who intends to keep control over his audience, the omnipotent author being a parallel to the omnipotent king. In any case, it must be treated from now on as a major Lafontainian creation.

La Fontaine wrote the verse dedication of the *Recueil de poésies chrétiennes et diverses,* published in 1671, to the young Prince de Conti (1661–85). The authorship of the *préface,* attributed by some scholars to La Fontaine (*O.D.,* 779–84), remains disputed. As Pierre Clarac pointed out, it is an important text, well written, but it does not bear the mark of La Fontaine's prose style (*O.D.,* 945–46). It seems to us that the strongly expressed pedagogical concern points to one of the Port-Royal scholars, possibly Pierre Nicole, as argued by Jules Brody.[33] It was natural for the Port-Royal promoters of the volume to ask La Fontaine to write the dedicatory epistle, since he had dedicated the first *Fables* in 1668 to another child, the dauphin. The Conti family was known for its Jansenist leanings.[34] One line in the dedication clearly indicates, by the use of the plural, that several persons collaborated in the process of selection and edition of the poems: "Ceux qui par leur travail l'ont mis en cet

état. . . ." (*O.D.*, 590; Those who have worked to put it together
. . .). The fact that austere Jansenists were involved in such an
undertaking is explained by La Fontaine: the selections are Christian
poetry and le "profane innocent," that is nonreligious texts, as long
as they conform to standards of propriety and decorum. The par-
ticipation of La Fontaine shows once more his versatility, his desire
to please and instruct all kinds of readers, and his friendly relations
with persons of letters of varied persuasion.

It is also clear that he shared the aesthetic notions of the *préface*,
rejecting rules and set standards as pedantic. He believed, like the
author of the *préface*, that judgment and taste are the best guides
in aesthetic matters.

It is also in 1671, in a volume entitled *Fables nouvelles et autres
poésies*, dedicated to the duc de Guise, son-in-law of Madame, dowager duchesse d'Orléans, of the household to which La Fontaine was
attached, that he published four *Elégies*. The date of their composition is not documented. Stylistically, they appear to us very close
to *Psyché* because of their mixture of pathos and humor.

The elegy was traditionally a poetic genre written in rhymed
couplets on themes of loss, mourning, and suffering. This is precisely
the case here: the poet sings of his amorous sufferings caused by
Clymène's indifference. The first *élégie* starts with an apostrophe to
Love: the poet asks the god what he has done to attract his wrath:

> Amour, que t'ai je fait? dis-moi quel est mon crime:
> D'où vient que je te sers tous les jours de victime?
> . . . .
> N'es-tu pas satisfait des maux que j'ai soufferts?
> (*O.D.*, 601)

> (Love, what I have done to you? Tell me what my crime is:
> How come I am your constant victim?
> . . . .
> Are my sufferings not enough for you?)

The poet presents himself as an innocent victim. He does not appear
in the rest of the poem as a tragic figure however. A detailed
evocation of all his disappointments in love follows; it seems incre-
dible that such a series of misfortunes could have happened to the
same person: a definitely humorous overtone is thus created.[35] This

comical account of amorous disasters includes a lightly satirical gallery of feminine portraits. The poet's latest passion for Clymène is also unrequited since she is mourning a dead lover. The paradox is that, although capable of love,[36] she does not wish to respond to the poet's tender pleas. He then appears implicitly not only unfortunate but clumsy as a suitor. This light, self-deprecating treatment is unusual in such poetry.

The names used are fictional and poetic. Some commentators have tried to relate some of these misfortunes to episodes in La Fontaine's life: the mystery remains.[37] Is the Clymène of the *Elégies* the same person or persona as the one of the "comédie" *Clymène,* also published with the third part of the *Contes* in 1671? She is represented in *Clymène* as totally opposed to love; in the *Elégies,* she has loved.

The second *élégie* uses the traditional metaphor of the dangerous sea to represent misfortunes in love and emphasizes the vulnerability of the poet's heart; in spite of past sufferings, he is always making a new attempt: he paints himself again as an innocent victim, a truly submissive, courtly lover, and offers his sufferings and his death in homage to Clymène. Again, it seems difficult to take completely seriously such declarations and the same self-mocking undercurrent detected in the first elegy seems present.

The third poem uses the conventional topos of the rival. The poet has lost his taste for life, he cannot enjoy what were before pleasurable pursuits: friendships, love affairs, poetry. Although tempted to forget Clymène by pursuing a new love, he cannot adopt such a cure, so great is Clymène's attraction: he will die her slave. The fourth elegy speaks of jealousy as the ultimate torment; the rival causing his jealousy is the dead lover who had followed Clymène's advice and changed his love into friendship. The poet cannot do the same. Besides, now that this lover is dead, Clymène mourns for him as a woman in love.

The themes of the *élégies* are the traditional ones but are treated in a somewhat lighthearted manner, with some degree of self-mockery. The poet appears half-serious, half-joking, making fun of his woes. Although the *élégies* do not generate deep pathetic emotion, they possess a certain charm, precisely because of the unusual tone adopted by the poet in a conventional genre. He thus implicitly questions the validity of the conventions he is using, just as he questioned the separation and hierarchy of genres in *Psyché.*

When the dowager duchesse d'Orléans died in February 1672,

La Fontaine lost his position in her household. But he was to find a new patroness in Madame de la Sablière from 1673 until her death in 1693. This was a turning point in La Fontaine's life and the beginning of a very productive literary period.[38]

Chapter Six
The *Fables* of 1678–79

The Christian inspiration apparent in the contribution of La Fontaine to the *Recueil de poésies chrétiennes et diverses* and implicit in Psyché's discovery of altruistic love, did surface again in the "Poème de la captivité de saint Malc." Its dedication to the young cardinal de Bouillon, younger brother of the duke and nephew of Turenne was a gesture of loyalty and gratitude to the Bouillon family whose protection the poet certainly appreciated. Cardinal de Bouillon (1643–1715) had been elevated in 1669 to the rank of cardinal, a prince of the church, and in 1671, at the very young age of twenty-six, he was named Grand Aumônier de France; he was therefore making a brilliant career in the church. It was the tradition in aristocratic families that the older son establish the family name in the military, as did the duc de Bouillon, praised for his valor in the *Psyché* epistle addressed to his wife; and the younger son in the church. Cardinal de Bouillon was known for his friendly relations with the Jesuits. La Fontaine in his dedicatory epistle praised his piety, his cultivated literary taste, the purity of his life, and his wisdom. It was therefore fitting to dedicate to such a prelate, honored by the pope and the king, the story of a saint who had shown an heroic attachment to purity and chastity.

La Fontaine calls his poem an idyll: it deals with sacred and Christian love as *Adonis* dealt with human and pagan love, both stories taking place in country settings and written in the heroic style of alexandrine rhymed couplets. The poet acknowledges that he found the subject of his poem in a letter of Saint Jerome, translated by the Port-Royal scholar Arnauld d'Andilly in the first volume of his *Vies des saints pères du désert* (1647–53). This source was used again in La Fontaine's last fable, "Le Juge arbitre, l'hospitalier et le solitaire." Commentators do not agree on the religious tendency implicit in the poem. To some, the celebration of retreat away from the world, in a life devoted to piety and prayer seems very close to the ideal of the Port-Royal "solitaires." To others, the fact that the recipient of the poem was a prince of the church, closely associated with the Jesuits, would preclude the expression of any Jansenist sympathy on the part of the author. To us, the religious atmosphere and feeling emanating from the text is that of a fervent early Christianity, with its dedication to eremitic life and complete detachment from all earthly pursuits. It may very well be that at least some of the "solitaires" were trying to recapture this Golden Age of Christianity. At any rate, there is in the poem an aura of a far away, fabulous past.

It starts with an invocation to the Virgin, parallel to the invocation to the Muses found in epic or "heroic" works, but not suitable for a Christian subject. The hero, Malc, was educated in a solitary retreat by a holy man. When his parents die, he is tempted to get his inheritance and leaves, in spite of his mentor's advice. While traveling, his party, among which is a young bride, is attacked by Saracens. The young woman, who has made a vow of chastity, and Malc become prisoners and keep the herds of their Arab master who wants them to become husband and wife. To escape the temptation, Malc is about to commit suicide but is prevented from doing so by his companion. They decide to flee their cruel master who, in pursuing them, is killed by a lioness. The two saints reach a safe place, the young woman enters a monastery, and Malc lives as a hermit.

Although La Fontaine was probably writing during the same period some racy tales for the *Nouveaux Contes,* he did take his task seriously, according to Pierre Clarac; he thought over Saint Jerome's account and added much of his own, thus creating a work that bears his mark.[1] It offers pastoral and courtly scenes that remind the reader of d'Urfé's *L'Astrée;* however, as noted by Collinet, the poet cleverly adds a biblical touch to the pastoral scenes by the mention of cedars. For this critic, the poem as a whole remains uneven.[2]

The theme of the refusal of a legitimate human love for the higher one of God had been part of the Christian tradition since *The Life of Saint Alexis,* an early medieval hagiographical work. It had been treated in the seventeenth century by a major dramatist, Pierre Corneille, in his two martyr plays, *Polyeucte* (1643) and *Théodore* (1646). Both Clarac and Collinet note that it is in the specifically religious meditations that the poem reaches its greatest strength. In one of these passages, God's grace and blessings and the thanksgiving owed by humans are mentioned:

Sa grâce est notre guide ainsi que notre appui:
Nous ne persévérons dans le bien que par lui.
Allons nous acquitter de ce bienfait immense.

(O.D., 58)

(His grace is our guide and our strength:
We persevere in the right path only through Him.
Let us repay this extraordinary benefaction.)

This mention of grace may have led commentators to see a Jansenist influence; however, the beneficence of God and the call for thanksgiving is very much a central theme of the Psalms and therefore in the biblical tradition.

To us, this poem has the charm of some seventeenth-century religious paintings; at times it has the mysterious pastoral beauty of certain works by Claude Le Lorrain or the sweetness of Moreau's music for *Esther*. It certainly weaves a thread between the pagan *Adonis* and the last fable.[3]

La Fontaine's taste for diversification during the following years 1674–75 is evident in his collaboration with the composer and music director Lulli who was writing operas for the court. Louis XIV's favorite, Madame de Montespan and her sister Madame de Thiange, who did not like Lulli's regular librettist, Quinault, recommended La Fontaine to the composer. He pretended to accept their recommendation and asked La Fontaine for the libretto of *Daphné,* which he turned down on the excuse that it was simply a pastoral play, not suited for a victorious king. In fact, he had arranged quietly to have Quinault work on another opera, *Thésée,* performed in January 1675 at the château of Saint-Germain. Furious, La Fontaine wrote a satire against Lulli, *Le Florentin,* denouncing his cupidity and dishonesty. It remained unpublished by him. Lulli (1633–87) was born in Florence and had made a brilliant career at the French court, having become Louis XIV's favorite composer and provider of entertainment. He obtained exclusive rights on musical productions, a privilege that hampered Molière in his last "comédies-ballets."

Daphné was in fact a conventional mythological play on a love theme. Since Louis XIV had recently conquered Franche-Comté, something of a more heroic nature was expected.[4] In a pique caused by his disappointment, La Fontaine attacked opera as an inferior mixture of all the arts in his letter to M. de Niert (*O.D.*, 617–20); Racine expressed a similar position in his *Préface d'Iphigénie* at about the same time. This fiasco did not, however, keep La Fontaine from the theatre; he wrote other operas, *Galatée* and *Astrée*, and an unfinished tragedy, *Achille.*[5]

It was important for his career and reputation to obtain the patronage of the king's favorite: he therefore dedicated the 1678 *Fables*, books 7 to 11, to Madame de Montespan. She and her sisters, Madame de Thiange and the abbess of Fontevrault, belonged to the illustrious family of the Mortemarts. Madame de Montespan (1641–1707), born Françoise-Athénais de Mortemart had beauty and wit; she contributed greatly to the brilliant and sophisticated atmosphere of the court between 1668 and 1680. Her children by the king were legitimized: it was for one of them, the duc du Maine, that Madame de Thiange had a toy, "la chambre du Sublime," made as a New Year gift in 1675. La Fontaine was represented in it with other writers, La Rochefoucauld, Madame de Lafayette, Bossuet, Boileau, and Racine. It is generally thought that La Fontaine was introduced to the Mortemart sisters by La Rochefoucauld and Madame de Lafayette.

The second collection of *Fables*, the actual Books 7 to 11 was published in 1678–79 and remains, as Collinet has pointed out, the poet's supreme achievement.[6] Having stated the poetics of the genre in the *préface* of 1668, La Fontaine probably thought that a short and simple *Avertissement* would suffice. Again a concern for variety in subject matter and style is expressed. The poet says that he has developed the circumstances more fully in the narrations and has used a new source book, the Indian Pilpay, in translation,[7] as well as others.

The verse dedication to Madame de Montespan praises the fable as a genre: it must be considered a gift from the gods and Aesop as a wise man who should be raised to the rank of deity. Fables possess a magic spell that can captivate hearts and minds: La Fontaine is paving the way for his famous fable "Le Pouvoir des fables" (8,4).

Madame de Montespan, addressed under the poetic name of Olympe, perhaps because as Jupiter's favorite she was a resident of Olympus, is compared to Aesop: by her brilliant and witty conversation, she too casts a spell. Olympe's protection will insure immortality to his work.

After such lavish praise and such a courtly introduction, the first fable creates an effect of contrast. After the Olympian world of beauty, grace, and glory, the poet presents to his readers the real world of sickness, death, superstitious beliefs, and injustice in one of the best known and most powerful fables, chosen as an opening because of its dramatic qualities. The plague, a terrible illness, most feared in medieval and early modern times, wages war against the animals. All are affected and lose their taste for life if not life itself. It is seen as a punishment from heaven for their sins and desperate measures are in order. The archaic, primitive view that a sacrifice to the deity will appease its wrath is put forward by the lion represented as a king consulting his council. He thinks that the most guilty among them should be offered as an expiatory victim. The guilt of each is then determined according to his or her strength and power; the weakest, the donkey, is judged to be the guilty one. The moral is very terse:

> Selon que vous serez puissant ou misérable,
> Les jugements de cour vous rendront blanc ou noir.
> ("Les Animaux malades de la peste," 7, 1, *Fables* 180)

> (And so, as you are weak or are invincible,
> The courts says white is black or that black crimes are white.
> "The Animals Sick of the Plague," 7, 1, p. 144)

In spite of such a cynical conclusion, the fable offers a great variety of diction and is very successful as a poetic creation. The introduction presenting the ravages of the plague has the dignity and grandeur of the epic. The description of the animals' sufferings has an elegiac quality:

> Les Tourterelles se fuyaient:
> Plus d'amour, partant plus de joie.
> (7, 1, *Fables,* 179)

> (The demoralized doves scattered
> And love starved; life was moribund.
> 7, 1, 143)

A black comedy follows, with the lion holding council, enlivened by comic effects: the word "le berger" is detached in a single short line of three syllables from the rest of the lion's speech, creating an imitation of his gobbling up the unfortunate shepherd. A witty satire of court manners comes out in the speeches of the various animals: thus the fox argues that it was an honor for the sheep to be killed and devoured by the lion. The shepherd deserved his fate because of human arrogance: people think of themselves as superior to animals. The donkey's confession is comical since his "sin" is so harmless; the disproportion between crime and punishment creates a strikingly ironic effect and the fable ends on a tragic note: the sacrifice of the least guilty.

Social satire is seen again in "Le Rat qui s'est retiré du monde" (7, 3). The rat refuses to contribute to a community project of national importance, the defense of their capital, with the fabulous name of Ratopolis. The editor of the *Fables*, Georges Couton, links it to a contemporary event, the regular clergy's protest against a heavy contribution of three hundred thousand pounds voted by the Assembly of the Clergy of France to help Louis XIV finance his war against Holland (*Fables*, 467, n. 1). The rat, precisely, has retired in a huge Holland cheese, a comfortable and nourishing retreat. Monks in popular literature, and in La Fontaine's *Contes* were portrayed as self-indulgent and lecherous. Here, however, the poet says that the rat could not represent a monk, since monks are supposed to be charitable, but an oriental equivalent, a "dervis": he is joking, of course.

The "fable-double," "Le Héron" and "La Fille" elaborates on the theme of "Contre ceux qui ont le goût difficile," going from the realm of literary taste to the even more personal one of food and marriage. The poet emphasizes the vanity and self-confidence of both the bird and the young woman, under the guise of fastidiousness. The transition between the two fables is provided by the moral, placed in the middle, applying to both exempla:

> Ne soyons pas si difficiles:
> Les plus accommodants ce sont les plus habiles:
> ....
>   ce n'est pas aux Hérons
> Que je parle; écoutez, humains, un autre
>   conte;
> Vous verrez que chez vous j'ai puisé ces leçons.
>   ("Le Héron," "La Fille," 7, 4, *Fables*, 183)

> (Don't be irreconcilable;
> The better the mind is, the more adaptable.
> ....
> Maxims we neglect—meant for men and not herons alone;
> So be warned. Friends, I have something else to relate
> Which certainly could instruct almost anyone.
>   "The Heron," 7, 4, p. 148)

Both Leo Spitzer and Patrick Dandrey have commented on the skill
of La Fontaine in this transition.[8] The source of inspiration for these
twin fables has been discussed in the context of the general subject
of the pairing of fables dealing with a similar topic.[9] Collinet points
out that "La Fille" at the beginning of book 7 appears like an echo
of "La Jeune Veuve" at the conclusion of book 6. In a later study,
the critic acknowledges that the type of the hard-to-please woman,
reduced in the end to taking an unattractive husband, belongs to
a long tradition; but he wonders if there was a contemporary cor-
relative that would provide a key to the fable. He proposes "la
Grande Mademoiselle" (1627–93), Gaston d'Orléans's daughter by
his first wife, Marie de Bourbon-Montpensier, first cousin to Louis
XIV, who had forbidden her marriage to Lauzun eight years before
the publication of the fable.[10] This very rich princess had many
suitors, but she had turned them down, probably hoping to marry
the king himself, at least until the Fronde. Finally, she was glad
enough to accept an obscure member of the provincial aristocracy,
Lauzun, unattractive in his physical appearance as well as in his
personality, according to contemporary documents:

> Celle-ci fit un choix qu'on n'aurait jamais cru,
> Se trouvant à la fin tout aise et tout heureuse
> De rencontrer un malotru.
>   ("La Fille," 7, 4, *Fables,* 184)

> It can spur a fool too spoiled for any use,
> To do what once would have been the surprise of her life—
> Gladly seize in the end one whom no one would choose,
> And be an uncouth fellow's wife.
>   "The Haughty Lass," 7, 5, p. 149)

The dangers of expressing a frank opinion to powerful individuals
are presented in "La Cour du lion": the bear is dispatched to Hades

for having been too open in his criticism; the monkey, too syco-phantic, is not appreciated either. The fox finds an excuse for not stating an opinion and gets away with it. The thread of social satire goes on throughout the collection.

One of the most famous of all La Fontaine's fables is "La Laitière et le pot au lait," which offers in an epilogue a charming personal confession by the poet and a meditation on the weakness of human nature in which he abundantly shares. The peasant woman taking her jug of milk to market and dreaming of a fortune is Everyman, including La Fontaine. Of course, lost in her dreams, she forgets herself, jumps for joy, and spills the milk. She contemplates with sorrow her vanished fortune and goes home with the prospect of a sound beating from her husband.

The milkmaid joins kings, real and fictional, bringing up the notion of a universal tendency to live in a fantasy world; the tran-sition between the daydreams of the milkmaid and those of most people, including the poet's, has been studied.[11] Those personal dreams of glory recall those of Matamore in Corneille's *L'Illusion comique* and are indeed comical by their very hyperbolic nature. The word "accident" used in a philosophical sense parallels the real accident that befell the milkmaid and the last line has fittingly become a proverb: "Quelque accident fait-il que je rentre en moi-même; Je suis gros Jean comme devant" (*"La Laitière et le pot au lait,"* 7, 9, *Fables,* 191) cutting the dreamer down to size, a simple, naive countryman, Big John as before. This lucid appraisal of oneself is very refreshing after the vanity and self-delusion of the heron and the "haughty lass."

"Le Curé et le mort" is based, like some of the *Contes* and *Fables,* on a contemporary event, documented by a letter of Madame de Sévigné of 26 February 1672. It starts: "M. de Boufflers killed a man after his death" (*Fables,* 473, n. 1). Couton notes that "La Laitière et le pot au lait" and "Le Curé et le mort," dealing with dreams of fortune brutally interrupted, are in fact twin fables like "Le Héron" and "La Fille"; however La Fontaine did not put them together. It does not seem that it was for reasons of decorum. The priest, with the money earned in the funeral service, thinks of sensual pleasures: he plans to buy a cask of the best local wine and dresses for his niece and her maid. The very name of the pastor, Jean Chouart was used by Rabelais with a phallic connotation (*Fables,* 473–74, n. 3). Here, however, the bawdy implications are veiled enough not to shock. The black humor comes out in a wonderful manner: the coffin slides and kills the priest:

> Le paroissien en plomb entraîne son Pasteur;
> Notre Curé suit son Seigneur;
> ("Le Curé et le mort," 7, 10, *Fables,* 192)

> The weighty parishioner struck his shepherd hard;
> Our shepherd must follow his over-lord.
> "The Curé and the Corpse," 7, 11, p. 157)

An excellent analysis of this fable's ironic features is given by Richard Danner who points out that "the basic event of the fable is clearly ironic" as well as the final reversal. Sensitive to the modern reader-response approach, he concludes: "The one who would lead has himself been led; the apparent master of the situation has been mastered. The ultimate possessors turn out to be the fabulist/narrator and his mute but mentally active accomplice-in-irony, the reader."[12]

In "Les Deux Coqs," epic tradition is used to create a comic and parodic effect. Love caused the fall of Troy as it caused the fight between two roosters for a hen: "Amour, tu perdis Troie . . . . " ("Les Deux Coqs," 7, 12, *Fables,* 195). The outcome, again, is ironic: the victorious hero, proud of his triumph, sings so loudly that he is seized by a vulture. It reminds the reader of "La Grenouille et le rat" in which the kite takes off with the two smaller animals (4, 11), thus having meat and fish for its supper.

The concluding fable, "Un Animal dans la lune" is an important one. It shows the poet sharing the scientific interests of his time in astronomy and curious about the discoveries made through the use of the telescope and more broadly in philosophical problems of perception and knowledge. La Fontaine may have known a satirical poem written in England by Samuel Butler (1612–80) against the Royal Society, a scientific academy founded in 1660 and presided over since 1671 by Newton, through his exiled friend Saint-Evremond (*Fables,* 480, n. 1). We would agree with Couton that the philosophers La Fontaine has in mind are the two major French thinkers of the seventeenth century, Descartes and Gassendi. The interest and admiration of the poet for Descartes is strongly expressed in his "Discours à Mme de La Sablière":

> Descartes, ce mortel dont on eût fait un Dieu
> Chez les Païens, et qui tient le milieu
> Entre l'homme et l'esprit. . . .
>
> > (9, *Fables*, 267)

> (Descartes, a man whom heathen would have made a god
> A sort of mean between spirit overhead
> And man below. . . .
>
> > 9, p. 230)

The publication of *La Recherche de la vérité* by the Cartesian philos-opher Malebranche (1674 and 1675) had reactivated the debate on how far we could trust our perceptions. La Fontaine states forth-rightly that both sides are right: circumstances such as distance, environment, organ, or instrument of perception must be taken into consideration. This is a rationalist and relativist view, placed as a closing statement to Book 7.

The example chosen to illustrate this view is, fittingly, the moon seen through a telescope. The mountainous surface of the moon presents to the naked eye the image of a woman's face: this is simply a visual illusion. Some time ago, in England, scientists looking through a telescope thought they had seen a new animal on the moon. King Charles II was intrigued by the news. Superstitious predictions came out: it was the sign of a major event, an armed conflict probably. The mysterious sign was in fact a mouse found between the lenses of the telescope. The discovery made people laugh.

The transition from this philosophical topic to the next one, the political problem of war and peace might have seemed difficult. Leo Spitzer believes that La Fontaine discovered the "Ariadne's thread" that leads from the anecdote of the mouse in the telescope and the Royal Society of London to the English king and the establishment of a peace that allows arts and sciences to flourish: "To blur the impression that he wanted to lecture his own king, Louis XIV, with the panegyric of the English monarch, La Fontaine invented an extremely subtle transition. He puts out the idea that victory . . . is always on the French side. . . . Charles is invoked as a *channel* of peace, not as an opponent of Louis XIV."[13]

La Fontaine meditates on the English people's good fortune: they can devote their time and energy to scientific pursuits, while France is waging war. To be sure, it has brought to Louis XIV the laurels of victory, but his people wish for peace. The poet hopes that the English king will serve as a mediator and bring some agreement between the countries at war. The very actual question of France's foreign policy is thus tactfully presented: Louis XIV's victories are praised but the desire of the nation for peace clearly suggested. Did La Fontaine hope that Madame de Montespan would find these arguments persuasive and convince her royal lover of that very real desire?

Book 8 has been characterized as "the Epicurean book of the *Fables*" by Georges Couton.[14] Epicurean views are in fact scattered throughout the *Fables:* it is a recurrent theme and one of the threads that link the various books together. The first fable, "La Mort et le mourant," recalls "La Mort et le bûcheron" (1, 16): whenever faced with death, the individual clings to life, philosophical considerations notwithstanding. Epicurean thought is found in the concluding remark:

> Je voudrais qu'à cet âge
> On sortît de la vie ainsi que d'un banquet,
> Remerciant son hôte et qu'on fît son paquet.
> ("La Mort et le mourant," 8, 1, *Fables,* 206)

> (When our powers are failing us,
> Let us fare as from a feast; but like guests, first delay,
> Thank our host for his best and then be on our way.
> "Death and the Dying," 8, 1, p. 170)

The concern with war, seen in the final fable of book 7 comes up again: death and the sufferings of many young people on the battlefield are contrasted with biting irony to the fears of elderly people who have nothing to lose: "Le plus semblable aux morts meurt le plus à regret." (8, 1, *Fables,* 206; That most like the dead are those most loath to die. 8, 1, p. 170).

"Le Savetier et le financier" is part of a series, according to Couton, designed to teach a lesson of moderation, praising the Horatian *aurea mediocritas*: after a lesson on how to die, a lesson on how to live.[15] The charm of this fable comes from the comic contrast between the man living a simple life, happy in his work, and the rich man, so worried about his fortune that he is unable to enjoy it. The two individuals are presented in a lively dialog, which emphasizes the comic aspect. The fable probably alludes to the social realities of the period: the rise of a wealthy upper middle class that was changing the traditional social structures. But its major thrust is the destructive power of money, a perennial theme. As soon as the cobbler possesses money, he loses his peace of mind and his "joie de vivre." This radical change is expressed in comic terms:

> Tout le jour il avait l'oeil au guet; Et la nuit,
>   Si quelque chat faisait du bruit,
> Le chat prenait l'argent. . . .
>   ("Le Savetier et le financier," 8, 2, *Fables*, 208)

> (Both ears and eyes were alert all day, and at night,
>   If so much as a cat trod light,
> He thought it would thieve his fund.
>   "The Cobbler and the Financier," 8, 2, p. 172)

In "Le Pouvoir des fables," La Fontaine comes back to his constant preoccupation with his art and his freedom of choice in the literary domain, noticed in the 1668 *Fables* ("Simonide préservé par les dieux," "Contre ceux qui ont le goût difficile," "Le Meunier, son fils et l'âne") It is dedicated to M. de Barillon, ambassador of France to the English court (from 1677 to 1688): again here La Fontaine's concern with France's foreign policy and for peace is apparent, as in "Un Animal dans la lune." The first part of the fable, addressed to the French ambassador is directly linked to a crucial problem, that of a European coalition against France and the possible loss of Charles II of England as an ally. The close family relationship between the Bourbons and the Stuarts seemed a stabilizing factor in the balance of power in Europe.[16] Again, the poet presents tactfully the difficult position of Louis XIV, comparing him to Hercules fighting the Hydra of Lerna, one of the twelve labors of Hercules in Greek mythology. The poet hopes that Barillon, a seasoned diplomat with consummate skill in the art of persuasion, will convince the English king to continue his support to France. If he succeeds, La Fontaine will sacrifice one hundred sheep and burn incense in thanksgiving. The mythological and the pagan elements are humorously woven with the real, contemporary dilemma of war and peace, attenuating perhaps its tragic implications, but also raising the protagonists, Louis XIV and his representative at the Court of Saint James, to the level of demigods.

The skillful transition between the first and the second part hinges
on the power of persuasion, possessed by the French ambassador,
and essential to the didactic purpose of the fable. There are in fact
three stages, since the poem opens with an orator unable to persuade
his audience by stating the truth and then having recourse to a
fable. The appearance of the fable proper is delayed, a trick very
common in the theater where the entrance of the protagonist is
sometimes delayed for effect. At the beginning of the second part,
La Fontaine is in fact recounting a story, that of a speech made by
an orator to the Athenians threatened by the conquests of Philip of
Macedonia. They do not listen until he mentions the trip that the
goddess Ceres made with an eel and a swallow: this is the narrative
trap that gives the narrator the power to manipulate his audience.[17]

The Athenians, awakened by the reproach of the orator, modeled
probably after Demosthenes, pay full attention to what he has to
say. The conclusion is very apt. The poet speaks in his own name,
admitting willingly that he shares in human frailty, just as he did
in "La Laitière et le pot au lait":

> Nous sommes tous d'Athène en ce point, et moi-
>   même,
> Au moment que je fais cette moralité,
>   Si *Peau d'âne* m'était conté,
>   J'y prendrais un plaisir extrême. . . .
>   ("Le Pouvoir des Fables," 8, 4, *Fables,* 211)

> (All are Athenians; I am the same,
> Since the moment The Ass's Skin commences,
>   Away with appearances;
>   I am enraptured, really am.
>   "The Power of Fables," 8, 4, p. 175)

"Le Rat et l'huître" has recently attracted the attention of La
Fontaine scholars, with good reason, for it is a delightful fable that
introduces a theme taken up again in "Les Deux Pigeons," the desire
to leave one's home and see the world, with the attendant dangers
in such adventures. The rat, an inexperienced youth, was not what
the French call "un rat de bibliothèque", a bookworm: he had neither
book-learning nor direct experience of the world; no wonder he was
caught when attracted by the prospect of a good meal. The lesson
is presented both at the moral and the epistemological levels: greed

leads the rat to its untimely end, like the frog in "La Grenouille et le rat" (4, 11), but also "curiosity killed the cat"; intellectual curiosity, like the tongue, can be the best or the worst thing. The relativist view noted before prevails here again.

For Odette de Mourgues, the rat represents stupidity and immaturity, vanity, and self-satisfaction: we are very close to la Rochefoucauld's views. But the rat has weaknesses not only of character, but also of intelligence. He jumps to conclusions and makes false generalizations, shows scorn for his elders, and manifests the arrogance of ignorance, that of the half-educated. He lacks judgment, thinking the world and the oyster made for him. What makes this tale of immaturity and its dire consequences funny is the contrast between two styles, one noble, mythological, and majestic, the other familiar and realistic. This view is shared by Alain Seznec.[18]

Michael Vincent reads the fable as a palimpsest. The rat, so eager for adventures, is a quixotic figure recalling the protagonists of the adventure novels, while the oyster with her white, mother-of-pearl flesh, her voluptuous yawn and abandon is very close to the women-nymphs of the *romans galants,* in particular to La Fontaine's Aminte in *Le Songe de Vaux* and Psyché. In the fable, the motif of the stolen kiss becomes a deadly embrace, a trap. The reader, carried away by memories of the former texts, is caught in the trap, like the rat.[19]

Collinet compared the fable with its newly discovered source and shows how the poet developed the narrative, the characters, and even the moral, which he sees, as we do, as a foreshadowing of "Les Deux Pigeons."[20] Danner finds the moral somewhat superfluous for a modern reader, the last sentence of the narrative proper, "et voilà ce que fait l'ignorance," is closural enough. He recognizes the unmistakable ironic structure of the "wry reversal of subject and object" where the intended food consumes the would-be consumer.[21]

Friendship, again like Aesop's tongues, can be a double-edged sword, can kill or save, as we see in two succeeding fables, "L'Ours et l'amateur des jardins" and "Les Deux Amis" (8, 10 and 11). La Fontaine himself was very sensitive to the value of friendship, as seen in his "Discours à Mme de La Sablière." All major human feelings, emotions, and passions are certainly present in the *Fables.* Love appears in humorous form in "Tircis et Amarante" (8, 13), dedicated to the young Mademoiselle de Sillery, a niece of La Rochefoucauld, but in a far deeper, more personal guise in "Les Deux Pigeons."

Social satire reappears in "Les Obsèques de la lionne," a fable
dealing, as "La Cour du lion" (7, 6), with the dangers of life at
court, but with a more biting denunciation of hypocrisy and sy-
cophancy and a remark representing the human being as an autom-
aton, a preview of the discussions developed in the "Discours à Mme
de La Sablière": ironically it is men, the courtiers, not animals who
act as well-oiled mechanisms: "On dirait qu'un esprit anime mille
corps; / C'est bien là que les gens sont de simples ressorts" (Les
Obsèques de la lionne," 8, 14, *Fables,* 222).

We have seen in book 8 the theme of the desire for experience
and discovery, also that of love and friendship. La Fontaine combines
them in one of the most successful fables of book 9, "Les Deux
Pigeons," often anthologized. The fable again, is in two parts, the
first dealing with doves, the second becoming a lyrical meditation
where the poet speaks in his own name.

The first line presents a loving couple of birds: "Deux Pigeons
s'aimaient d'amour tendre" ("Les Deux Pigeons," 9, 2, *Fables,* 245).
One of them gets bored with a quiet, uneventful, if happy home
life and is foolish enough to decide to undertake a trip in faraway
lands, in spite of his mate's objections and loving concern for his
safety and comfort. All the dire predictions, announced by a passing
crow and the expected anxiety dreams of the mate are realized for
the traveler who is lucky enough to barely make it home, where,
of course, a sweet reunion awaits him.

The second part starts with an apostrophe to "happy lovers" who
should learn to know and appreciate each other rather than look for
diversity and novelty in the world outside. Personal reflexions follow:
the poet's happiest moments were those of his first love: will he
ever recapture such felicity?

This very rich text has attracted a lot of comments. Doves are,
of course, traditionally used as an allegory of love. One should note,
however, that in French the word used metaphorically is *tourterelles,*
turtle doves, not *pigeons* which is a far more familiar, poultry yard
term. La Fontaine thus brings his animal characters down to earth,
to the everyday level. It is well known that "mon frère" and "ma
soeur" are used to indicate tender love between man and woman,
from the medieval to the modern expression of tender feelings. The
use of "nos gens," as noted by Leo Spitzer, is "both a familiar
humanisation of animal heroes *and* a preparation for *amants.*"[22] The
use of the masculine form of the adjective "cruel," "L'absence est

le plus grand des maux: / Non pas pour vous, cruel" (9, 2, *Fables,* 245), indicates that the departing dove is a male, the tender mate left at home, a female. Leo Spitzer mentions Dido and one could certainly see here the elegiac theme of "la femme abandonnée." Michael Vincent notes, however, that in the telling of the traveler's misfortunes, La Fontaine uses the term "volatile" in the feminine: the word had both genders in the seventeenth century, thus blurring the gender difference.[23] This suggests that La Fontaine intended a generalization: the seeker of adventures could be either member of a couple. Although the *conte* is told in a different key, in "Joconde," both husbands and wives sought adventures and experiences outside marriage. To us, the use of the feminine "volatile" appears as a factor of universalization of the desire to know, to experience. Vincent interprets the desire to travel as a need to have a story to tell, an allegory of literary creation, the irony being that "the story he will have to tell, is already encapsulated in the predictions of the first pigeon."[24] He also brings out the delicately veiled erotic allusions of the fable: "Bon soupé, bon gîte et le reste?" and the terms "envie, appas, plaisirs." We are certainly dealing with love in all its aspects. It is precisely of that kind of love, in its fullest sense that the aging poet is dreaming, evoking happy memories of his youth, projected in a pastoral fiction, a mythic Golden Age of perennial happiness.

"Le Gland et la citrouille" (9, 4) brings up the Providential motif, already present in "Jupiter et le métayer" (6, 4), and contrasts the presumptuous thinking and arrogance of humans with Providential order and wisdom.

La Fontaine's dislike for pedantic learning and others' lack of sensitivity to living things, animal or vegetable, already noticed in "Le Jardinier et son seigneur," appears forcefully in "L'Ecolier, le pédant et le maître d'un jardin." The satirical tone concerning bookish learning, school boys, and school masters reminds the reader of Montaigne and Molière. The lovely description of the garden with its blossoms and fruit according to the season, a gift of bountiful nature, is contrasted with the horde of barbarians, the schoolboys who ruin it; they are like the hunting party that destroyed the vegetable garden in "The Gardener and the Squire." It is even more heartbreaking here since the schoolmaster should control and instruct his charges but instead quotes Virgil and Cicero, showing off a meaningless learning.

Book 9 concludes with a lengthy piece, the "Discours à Madame de La Sablière," not to be confused with the speech bearing the same title, read by La Fontaine at his reception in the Académie française. It is addressed to the poet's patroness and friend for many years. A charming, pretty, and well-educated woman, she attracted in her salon a circle of sophisticated and independent minds, interested in philosophical and scientific matters, the most important of whom, according to René Jasinski, was François Bernier, Gassendi's disciple and popularizer, author of an *Abrégé de la philosophie de Gassendi* (a one-volume edition appeared in 1674, and eight volumes in 1678).[25]

In his introduction to his published edition of the *"Discours,"* Henri Busson points out that La Fontaine was interested in intellectual problems throughout his life. The question of animal intelligence was very much discussed because of the spread of Cartesian theories on the subject in the later part of the seventeenth century. While acknowledging the direct contacts La Fontaine had with Bernier, a close friend of Madame de La Sablière, Busson examined the possible influence of other members of her circle and well-known authors of philosophical treatises.

Antoine Menjot, a medical man like Bernier, uncle of Madame de La Sablière, was a regular visitor, as well as Marin Cureau de la Chambre. The Marquis de La Fare, the hostess's lover also had philosophical interests.[26] Intellectual questions had become very fashionable with the founding of the Royal Society in London and the Académie des Sciences in Paris in 1666. Anatomy, physiology, astronomy, and physics had become current subjects of inquiry in the 1670s, as one can see in Molière's *Femmes savantes.* These scientific interests must have played a part in La Fontaine's choice of topic for his "Discours." The examples illustrating animal intelligence are taken for the most part from contemporary sources, from accounts of travelers who had observed beavers, for example, in the New World.

Animal intelligence had been discussed since antiquity; among French thinkers, Montaigne's famous essay, his *Apologie de Raymond de Sebonde* (1580), was well known. But the topic assumed a renewed preeminence in the 1670s with the opposition of Descartes and Gassendi's views on the matter: we find an echo of these controversies in the *"Discours à Mme de La Sablière."*

After a very charming introduction, praising the lady under the poetic name of Iris, tactfully chosen since Iris was the messenger of the gods and Madame de La Sablière had acted as an emanation from Providence to La Fontaine, offering him a generous and stimulating hospitality. Iris, however, different from the majority of the mortals and immortals, refuses to be praised. She is too concerned with other subjects to think of herself, either important, scientific ones, or light, entertaining conversations with her friends. All subjects have their merits and usefulness, even the light ones. The poet will speak, however, "De certaine philosophie / Subtile, engageante et hardie" ("Discours," 9, *Fables,* 266; "of a certain philosophy subtle, attractive, and bold").

It is, of course, Descartes's theory of animals seen as automatons. La Fontaine was perfectly aware of the French philosopher's greatness, as noted earlier about "Un Animal dans la lune" and felt he had to give him, so to speak, a fair hearing. That is precisely what he does in presenting the Cartesian views (ll. 24–52, 53–68) that animals are machines, self-conscious thought being reserved only to humans in the creation.[27] Examples refuting these theories are presented under the guise of anecdotes illustrating the intelligence of animals: the stag, acting out of self-preservation, the partridge trying to save her young, the social instinct of the beavers, and the military art of the bobacks. For the beavers, La Fontaine used the works of Nicolas Denys, one of the pioneers in Acadia, a region of New France now part of Nova Scotia and New Brunswick in Canada, *Description géographique et historique des costes de l'Amérique septentrionale.*[28] For the bobacks, he mentions as his source the king of Poland, Jean Sobieski; modern scholars think he used probably Beauplan's *Description d'Ukranie,* published in Rouen and issued there and in Paris in 1660 and 1661.[29] By using military terms, La Fontaine makes the bobacks appear like human soldiers. Although "Bobacks and Marmots do not live in the manner described by La Fontaine and presumably by Sobieski," some playful fighting observed among them may have led to the inflated attribution of military art to these animals, says Beverly Ridgely who concludes that it is "observed reality . . . distorted by oral or written transmission."[30]

The reply of the Cartesians to those animal stories is that they show a "corporeal memory," built in the body. In humans, intelligence and will are distinct from the body and the cause of the body's movements; in humans alone does a spiritual principle exist.

La Fontaine's retort is the example of "Les Deux Rats, le renard et l'oeuf," which gives him the opportunity to protest: "Qu'on aille me soutenir, après un tel récit / Que les bêtes n'ont point d'esprit!" ("Discours," *Fables,* 270, ll. 197–98; "Let people claim, after such an account, that animals are mindless") and to present his own moderate position in agreement, as Busson has shown, with the views of theologians such as Pardies and Du Hamel as well as some Gassendist thinkers who recognize some psychic activity in animals but distinguish it from the purely rational and self-reflexive mental activities in humans. There is, according to La Fontaine, a thinking activity in animals similar to that existing in children. There would be then two kinds of "souls," one common to animals and humans, made of subtle "atoms," and a rational one, spiritual and immortal, given to humans alone. This, of course, could open the door to a materialistic philosophy and the negation of immortality. The fact that La Fontaine may have perceived the dangers inherent in Gassendist theories is that he uses the conditional in the presentation of his views.[31]

Besides and beyond the philosophical problem, there is a personal, deeply felt reaction of the poet towards the animal world. We stated earlier that brutality, bestiality, and insensitivity are often depicted in the *Fables* as characteristic of humans who therefore are hardly superior to animals. The example of "Les Deux Rats, le renard et l'oeuf" shows not only intelligence but invention on the part of the animals. The paradox of the "Discours," according to Alain Seznec, is that real animals, not used here as in other fables as allegories for human behavior, are acting in a rational and hence, human way.[32] Against the brute force of the human hunter, the stag and the partridge use intelligent stratagems, enhanced by a feeling of duty and sacrifice in the case of the partridge. Humans are not as clever builders as beavers, and the bobacks have adopted the ultimate human invention: warfare.[33]

Human cruelty to animals, which is the theme of the opening fable of book 10, provides the link between the two books. Critics have noted that La Fontaine chose a symbolic yet familiar animal, the serpent, usually feared by people and killed as potentially dangerous; and on the mythic level, a symbol of evil, the incarnation of the devil who has to be crushed.[34] But the *couleuvre* chosen by La Fontaine is a harmless type of snake. In spite of the fact that this particular serpent does not represent any danger to him, the man of the title, who is judged totally ungrateful and destructive by the cow—with the ox and the tree called in turn as witnesses—brutally kills the innocent serpent. The moral is very close to that of the famous fable "Le Loup et l'agneau" (1, 10):

> On en use ainsi chez les grands.
> La raison les offense; ils se mettent en tête
> Que tout est né pour eux, quadrupèdes, et gens,
> Et serpents.
> ("L'Homme et la couleuvre," 10, 1, *Fables,* 277)

> (Justice offends him. Existing for him—
>   snake,
> Animal, mankind; everything and everyone
>   Is his own.
> "The Man and the Serpent," 10, 1, p. 238)

Richard Danner also makes the connection with the early fable and points out "a similar, though more discursive impact at the end of 'L'Homme et la couleuvre'." The critic notes the ambiguity of the first half of the concluding line: " 'Parler de loin' is open to an array of interpretations. On a figurative level, 'parler de loin' suggests verbal remoteness or speaking with irony. Such a survival technique enables the stag of 'Les Obsèques de la lionne' (VII, p. 14) to save his hide. . . . There is no guarantee in the labyrinthine world of the *Fables,* however, that similar strategies would be adequate to save every character from the whims of the powerful: the snake . . . is doomed from the start."[35]

Henri Lafay acknowledges the validity of the advice to any one dealing with the powerful, "Parler de loin, ou bien se taire" (10, 1, *Fables,* 277; Withdraw, or take care that your words are not heard; 10, 1, p. 238), but applies it to the writer and the textual meaning of the fable itself. After the mythic connotation of the serpent with Satan in the Garden of Eden, there is a reversal from harmful to beneficial animality in the cow and the ox, a connotation of shade and abundance in the tree, with Virgilian overtones, so that animals and vegetation in the fable fulfill the function of civilizing influences. The text shows a human presence in nature, not expressed in words, but suggested: in the fables universe, humans are sensitive to their animal and vegetal environment. [36]

Danner has proposed for book 10 "the labyrinth hypothesis." In

"L'Homme et la couleuvre," it is the human mind that is perverted: "As the story develops, however, the derogatory epithet, *pervers,* projected on a path of ironic indirection, will in no way fit the snake. . . . The man's mental processes are plainly inverted; his thinking evokes the tangled circuit of a labyrinth."[37]

The next fable, "La Tortue et les deux canards," appears as an elaboration of the "mind as labyrinth metaphor." It "amusingly demonstrates the proposition" found in the last lines of "L'Homme et la couleuvre": "Si quelqu'un desserre les dents, / C'est un sot," (10, 1, *Fables,* 277).

The tortoise, precisely by opening her mouth, falls and thus shows she is a fool:

> Car lâchant le bâton en desserrant les dents,
> Elle tombe, elle crève aux pieds des regardants.
> Son indiscrétion de sa perte fut cause.
>   ("La Tortue et les deux canards," 10, 2, *Fables,* 278)

> (Lost the stick when she parted her beak, so went down,
> And her hard shell had shattered near those looking on.
> Folly had dealt her one of life's mortal blows.
>   "The Tortoise and the Two Ducks," 10, 2, p. 239)

This fable has received perceptive attention from David Lee Rubin and Richard Danner who have both analyzed its major theme, expressed with an echolike repetition in "sotte vanité et vaine curiosité." Rubin's interpretation of the strong term, "elle crève," is very much to the point: " 'Crever' means not only to die but to burst, and upon bursting, a turtle's shell releases its contents and becomes empty. The turtle thus suffers punishment in the image of her defect: for vacuousness, she becomes a void."[38]

In the "Discours à M. le duc La Rochefoucauld," sometimes entitled "Les Lapins" ("The Rabbits"), we have another instance of the close relationship and community of thought between the two writers. La Fontaine comes back to a comparison between humans and animals and speaks in the first person, expressing personal opinions: in spite of their supposed dominion over nature and superiority through reason, humans do not act differently from rabbits or animals in general; they are just as thoughtless as rabbits and just as ferocious as dogs defending their territory against other dogs.

In human society, everyone, including writers, tries to keep away any possible rival. The fable ends with a delicate homage to the duke who, like Madame de La Sablière, had the modesty and good taste to refuse praise, but the poet felt he owed him a debt since La Rochefoucauld had given him the topic.

In book 11, which concludes the 1678–79 collection, La Fontaine remembers his patroness, Madame de Montespan, and dedicates the second fable, "Les Dieux voulant instruire un fils de Jupiter" to the son of Louis XIV and Mme de Montespan, the duc du Maine to whom "la chambre du Sublime" had been given in 1675. He was a bright child of nine who had "l'esprit joint au désir de plaire" (wit and the desire to be liked): thus he was destined, through these gifts, to become a brilliant leader in French society.

The most famous fables in book 11 are "Le Songe d'un habitant du Mogol" and "Le Paysan du Danube." "Le Songe," like "Les Deux Pigeons" is in two parts, the second being a lyrical meditation on the joys of retreat, presented in allegorical form in the fable proper: a man from Mongolia, in the exotic Far East, saw in a dream a vizier enjoying the bliss of the Elysian fields, while a hermit was burning in the flames of Hell. The interpreter of dreams tells him that the hermit used to spend much time at court, flattering the viziers. The vizier, on the contrary, tried to get away from court. The second part is a hymn to the beauty and pleasures of a bucolic retreat: Virgilian echoes can be heard. In such a retreat, one can receive inspiration from the Muses and contemplate the stars, or more simply enjoy a peaceful sleep. The last two lines,

> Quand le moment viendra d'aller trouver les morts,
> J'aurai vécu sans soin, et mourrai sans remords.
> ("Le Songe d'un habitant du Mogol," 11, 4, *Fables,*
> 302)

> (. . . when changing the earth for Death's shores
> Cares have not soured me: I depart without remorse.
> "The Mogul's Dream," 11, 4, p. 262),

show again La Fontaine's Epicurean inspiration, so well defined by Roger Zuber: a pagan happiness, expressing the dream of a free-thinking, if not irreligious man.[39]

In "Le Paysan du Danube" reappears another thread of the *Fables,*

the political and social concern with justice and civil peace. We
noticed earlier how discreetly, but with great feeling nevertheless,
La Fontaine expressed the desire of the nation, ravaged by war, for
the peace England was enjoying. Georges Couton has well analyzed
the political innuendoes of the fable.[40] He has shown that the peasant
speech, if inspired by a Providential philosophy of history, also deals
with the perennial problems of imperialist policies, here those of
Rome, treated by Corneille in *Nicomède* and *Sophonisbe*. They express,
according to Couton, a reverse view of the Roman myth celebrating
the *pax romana* and the unification of Europe. The critic believes
that the poet was certainly aware of the policies of conquest and
devastation during the wars against Holland, of the excessive tax-
ation ordered by Louvois, and of the general desire for peace.

Marcel Gutwirth points out that the fable expresses the topoi of
the moral superiority of the subjugated nation and the just turna-
bout, the victor being destined to subjugation some day. The contrast between an empire representing civilization and one representing
barbarians is reversed in favor of the barbarians; however, their
representative is absorbed in the system: he is made a patrician.
The critic concludes that the fable, as a genre created by La Fontaine,
can accommodate an eloquent speech. But the eloquence of the
peasant is the opposite of rhetoric. He speaks on the level of nature.[41]

The *épilogue* indeed urges that through the Muse, the poet trans-
lates the many voices of nature:

> Car tout parle dans l'Univers;
> Il n'est rien qui n'ait son langage.
> (11, *Fables*, 311)

> (So that everywhere they are heard and understood,
> Each in his vernacular.
> Since all have speech however crude.
> 11, p. 271)

Almost two centuries before Baudelaire, La Fontaine sees the poet
as "celui . . . qui comprend sans effort le langage des fleurs et des
choses muettes" ("the person . . . who understands without effort
the language of flowers and of mute things") and nature as "un
temple où de vivants piliers laissent parfois sortir de confuses paroles"
("a temple where living pillars utter sometimes mysterious words").

With perfect modesty, he claims only to have opened the way and urges others to continue, to bring to perfection his undertaking. The epilogue of a volume dedicated to Louis XIV's favorite had to close on a note glorifying the victories of the king, which it dutifully does, but the dreams and accomplishments of the poet, as seen through books 7 to 11 were going in a very different direction.

Chapter Seven

The Academy:
The Last Works

The loyalty and attachment of La Fontaine to the Bouillons and in particular to the charming if discredited duchesse, who was compromised in the "affaire des poisons," (1680) led to his writing, at the request of his patroness, the "Poème du Quinquina," published under that title with other works by Denis Thierry and Claude Barbin in January 1682. This topic may seem strange to the modern reader but the request of a pretty woman who was also the wife of the poet's overlord in Château-Thierry was a powerful reason to undertake it; the poet may also have seen it as belonging to the same vein as his "Discours à Madame de La Sablière." Scientific and philosophical interests were extremely prominent in the 1670s and 80s among society people as well as specialists, a trend that would become more and more pronounced: we have seen it in the "Discours" and in a fable like "Un Animal dans la lune." La Fontaine apparently took his task seriously and composed a long poem of 635 lines in two cantos, written in *vers libres*.[1] He thought of himself as doing in French what the Latin poet Lucretius had done in his famous poem *De rerum natura,* a major source of Epicurean doctrines: he was creating a new genre, scientific and philosophical poetry.

In the opening section of the "Poème," La Fontaine addresses the duchesse de Bouillon under the name of "Uranie." Urania was the Muse of Astronomy and Geometry and, by extension, of scientific pursuits. She was invoked by the poet in his dedication of *Adonis* to Fouquet. "Fouquet, l'unique objet des faveurs d'Uranie . . ." (*O.D.,* 800, n. 5). She was represented clad in azur blue, with a crown of stars, surrounded by spheres and holding in her hand a compass. The seventeenth-century French painter Eustache Lesueur had represented her in a well-known painting: it was therefore a flattering *nom du Parnasse* (poetic name) for the duchesse de Bouillon. La Fontaine presents himself as her faithful knight:

C'est pour vous obéïr, et non par mon choix,
Qu'à des sujets profonds j'occupe mon génie,
Disciple de Lucrèce une seconde fois.

(*O.D.*, 62)

(It is to obey you, and not by choice
That I apply my talent to deep subjects,
As a disciple of Lucretius for the second time.)

Lucretius (98–55 B.C.) was considered the master of philosophical poetry; La Fontaine had tried his hand at it in his "Discours à Madame de La Sablière." In this new attempt, we see the interest of the period in medical questions. Descartes himself was interested in anatomy and physiology. The English doctor William Harvey (1578–1657) had discovered the circulation of the blood and controversies about the new medical discovery were very lively as one can see from Molière's *Malade imaginaire* (1673) where the playwright makes fun of the old-fashioned doctors who refuse to admit Harvey's theory, and the *Arrêt burlesque,* a satire against the Medical School of the University of Paris, written by Boileau, Bernier, Molière, and their group.[2]

Pharmacopeia was also being revised and extended to include, beyond the traditional medicinal plants, new chemical compounds based on antimony and mercury:

Tout mal a son remède au sein de la nature.
Nous n'avons qu'à chercher: de là nous sont venus
L'antimoine avec le mercure.
Trésors autrefois inconnus.
Le quin règne aujourd'hui: nos habiles s'en servent.
Quelques-uns encore conservent
Comme un point de religion,
L'intérêt de l'Ecole et leur opinion.
Ceux-là même y viendront. . . .

(*O.D.*, 71)

(Every disease has its remedy in Nature.
We have only to look for it: from this search have come
Antimony and mercury,
Treasures unknown in the past.
Quinine reigns today: our experts use it.

> Some keep still
> As a point of religion
> The interest of the Faculty of Medicine and its opinion.
> Even those will come to it. . . .

La Fontaine's views echo those of Molière and certainly represent, here again, a modernist, scientific position based on experimental discoveries, be they those of Harvey or of the Europeans cured of their fever by quinine, and rejecting the authority of the conservative Faculty of Medicine. We can see here, besides an experimental view, a Providential one: bountiful nature has provided a remedy for every kind of illness.

This preoccupation with new medication appears repeatedly in Madame de Sévigné's correspondence, worried about her daughter's health and anxious to have her try the new remedies. Such was the quinquina, extract of the bark of a tree growing in Peru, named "kina" by the Indians and brought to Europe by Jesuit missionaries in 1649. La Fontaine had met in the salon of Madame de La Sablière a doctor named Monginot, author of a treatise *De la guérison des fièvres par le quinquina*, published anonymously in 1679; he also used the Cartesian physicist Jacques Rohault's *Traité de physique*. The new remedy, containing the potent febrifuge, quinine, had performed cures that popularized it: the prince de Condé and the minister Colbert were successfully treated with it. An Englishman named Talbot had performed some spectacular cures: La Fontaine was thus treating a fashionable topic related to health problems of the time; fevers of various types were very frequent, and their treatment a major preoccupation.

The next step in La Fontaine's career was to be his election to the French Academy. Since its foundation by Cardinal Richelieu in 1635, election to the academy was considered the crowning of a literary career, the definitive consecration. The death of Colbert in September 1683 had left a seat vacant. La Fontaine had enough friends in the company to have a plurality of votes. According to Charles Perrault, the poet had promised in a letter to a prelate of the company not to write any more *contes*.[3] Louis XIV wished his historiographer Boileau to be elected. According to Louis Racine, son of the playwright, when La Fontaine asked Boileau whether he would run against him, the author of the *Satires* assured him he would not put his name forward; however, he did receive a few votes.[4] La Fontaine was elected in November 1683, in spite of the opposition of Toussaint Rose, "secrétaire de la main" to the king, and an exchange of biting remarks with Benserade. The king delayed in giving his approval to the election. In January 1684, La Fontaine's "Ballade au Roi" was published in the *Mercure galant*, a fashionable periodical. It celebrates the king as a victorious and magnanimous hero, comparing him to the Scipios, Caesar, and Augustus. The *envoi* contains a veiled reference to the *Contes* with a promise to accept the advice of his critics. It was probably written after the November election to the academy, to convince Louis XIV that there was no reason to withhold his approval. At any rate, in April 1684, when another vacancy provided the opportunity for the election of Boileau, the king gave his approval to La Fontaine's. In May 1684, he was received as a new member and according to custom read a speech thanking the company. In that speech, he praised its role in the maintenance of the purity of the French language and literature: "Vous me recevez en un corps où non seulement on apprend à arranger les paroles; on y apprend aussi les paroles mêmes, leur vrai usage, toute leur beauté et leur force." (*O.D.*, 640; You welcome me in a company where one learns not only to put words together; one learns there also the words themselves, all their beauty and their strength.) This was an allusion to one of the major undertakings of the academy, its dictionary, published for the first time in 1694. La Fontaine dutifully fulfilled the task of any newly elected member to praise the king, the founder of the academy, Cardinal Richelieu, the latter's successor, Chancelier Séguier and his predecessor, in La Fontaine's case, Colbert. The latter passage was short and perfunctory: La Fontaine probably remembered him as responsible for the fall of his first patron, Fouquet.

In his reply the abbé de La Chambre, director of the academy, acknowledged the well-deserved reputation of the new member and gave a very good definition of his original genius: "Elle [l'Académie] reconnaît en vous un génie aisé, facile, plein de délicatesse et de naïveté, quelque chose d'original, et qui, dans sa simplicité apparente et sous un air négligé, renferme de grands trésors et de grandes beautés. (*O.D.*, 980; It recognizes in you an easygoing, flexible genius, full of delicacy and spontaneity, something original and which in its apparent simplicity and under relaxed appearance contains great treasures and priceless beauties.) One could not give a better summation of the special qualities that make La Fontaine a unique poet.

According to custom, some unpublished texts were read: La Fontaine read his second "Discours à Madame de La Sablière," thus proclaiming his gratitude, friendship, and admiration to the charming and generous hostess who continued to take care of him until she died in 1693, although by then she had converted and was spending most of her time in charitable work. This second "Discours" is a charming and moving confession of the poet in his sixties, quite an elderly person by seventeenth-century standards, of his character weaknesses, and his life's shortcomings. We noticed in the first fable, "La Cigale et la fourmi," the concern with time: it is expressed here in personal terms. The poet thinks of the time he has wasted. His friend, Iris (Madame de La Sablière) has used it wisely:

> Mais qui vois-je que vous sagement s'en servir?
> Si quelques-uns l'ont fait, je ne suis pas du nombre;
> Des solides plaisirs je n'ai suivi que l'ombre. . . .
>
> (O.D., 644)

> (But whom do I see but you use it [time] wisely?
> If some have done so, I am not one of them;
> I have followed only the shadow of worthwhile endeavors.)

He confesses that he has spent his time foolishly, joking, talking, reading novels, and gambling, a common weakness in the seventeenth and eighteenth centuries. If he were sensible, he would follow Iris's advice—at least in part: complete detachment would be too much of an effort for him. He is not steadfast by nature, but restless and always ready for a change. This is true not only in his personal life but in his artistic endeavors as well. He admits to be

> Papillon du Parnasse, et semblable aux abeilles
> . . . .
> Je suis chose légère, et vole à tout sujet;
> Je vais de fleur en fleur, et d'objet en objet. . . .
>
> (O.D., 645)

(Butterfly from Parnassus and very much like bees
. . . .

I am a creature of the air and fly at any occasion;
I go from one flower to the next and from one object of love to the
  next. . . .)

He has not concentrated his efforts in one genre, has been flighty
in poetry as in love. He has been the slave of two tyrants: love and
the desire for reputation. Iris could show him how to really live,
to enjoy solid pleasures, honor God, stop chasing women, and
cultivate self-knowledge. It will take La Fontaine almost another
ten years to reach this supreme conversion.

The lucidity with which the poet judges himself is endearing.
His admitted failure in his personal life did not prevent him from
having loyal friends and admirers until the end of his life. In his
artistic pursuits, variety and change were probably stimulating and
enriching. The *Fables* would not be what they are if La Fontaine
had not tried his hand at many genres and styles.

1685 saw the publication of the *Ouvrages de prose et de poésie des
sieurs de Maucroix et de La Fontaine,* containing a few *contes,* two
poems, "Philémon et Baucis" and "Les Filles de Minée," and eleven
new fables. These reappear in book 12 of the *Fables* and will be
discussed later.

The famous "Querelle des Anciens et des Modernes" had been
brewing since 1680. It was not altogether a recent issue. Since the
beginning of the seventeenth century, various writers had expressed
feelings of independence from classical models and claimed that they
were free to modify traditional forms, to follow their inspiration,
and to give a voice to contemporary preoccupations: such were d'Urfé
and Charles Sorel for the novel, Théophile de Viau and Saint-Amant
for poetry, Corneille for the theater. At the same time, modern
philosophers, such as Descartes and Pascal, by using scientific meth-
ods and applying rational criticism to accepted notions had brought
about a new way of thinking and a belief in discovery and progress.
A first episode of the quarrel centered around the question of the
use of Christian themes and characters, as opposed to mythological,
pagan ones, in poetry and in literature in general. Boileau con-
demned such use in his *Art poétique* in 1674, considering it unsuitable
and Desmarets de Saint-Sorlin, author of a Christian epic, *Clovis*
(1654), replied to him in 1675 in his *Défense de la poésie et de la
langue françaises.*

When at a meeting of the French Academy on January 1687

Charles Perrault read his poem *Le Siècle de Louis le Grand,* in which
he placed the productions of the reign of Louis XIV above those of
Augustus, Boileau made some indignant protestations: from then
on the quarrel entered its active phase. La Fontaine's position was
delicate since he was on friendly terms with both antagonists. Although favoring the "anciens," he was always opposed to pedantic
learning and abstruse expression. In his letter to Racine of 6 June
1686 he had criticized Ronsard for having spoiled the charm of
Greek and Latin texts by using them as a pedant rather than as a
poet (*O.D.,* 657). La Fontaine decided diplomatically to address the
epître expressing his views to Pierre-Daniel Huet (1630–1721), a
very scholarly and dignified prelate, respected for his learning and
for his official position as assistant to Bossuet in the dauphin's
education since 1670. Huet could certainly be considered above the
bitter attacks from each side and a fair and wise arbitrator.

The "Epître à Huet," was obviously an answer to Perrault's *Siècle
de Louis le Grand,* published with an official permission dated 5
February 1687. It must have been written in haste, between 27
January, the date of Perrault's reading, and 5 February, so much
so that Jean-Pierre Collinet wonders with good reason whether it
had not been composed much before that, offered to Huet as early
as 1674 in an unpublished form and revised for publication in 1687.[5]

In his introduction, La Fontaine mentions Quintilian, the celebrated ancient rhetorician who still enjoyed great influence in humanist and rhetorical training. He presents the general opinion of
his time and of the "modernes": arts are flourishing in France:

> La France excelle aux arts, ils y fleurissent tous;
> . . . .
> Les Romains et les Grecs sont-ils seuls excellents?
>   (*O.D.,* 647)

> France excels in the arts, they all thrive there;
> . . . .
> Are Romans and Greeks alone excellent?

La Fontaine admits that a close, slavish imitation is not productive,
hence the famous declaration: "Mon imitation n'est point un es-
clavage. . . . (*O.D.,* 648; My imitation is not slavery). He men-

tions his favorite authors whom he considers his masters: Terence, Horace, Homer, Virgil. He did, in his youth, take a modern author as a model, but realized it was dangerous because his unnamed model's style was too affected. He prefers for himself and recommends to others a natural style (*O.D.*, 649). His admiration for the great geniuses of antiquity does not prevent him from appreciating the modern writers, not only French but Italian as well: Ariosto, Tasso, Machiavelli, Boccaccio: one recognizes here the Italian sources of the *Contes*. La Fontaine's tastes were truly catholic: "J'en lis qui sont du Nord, et qui sont du Midi." (*O.D.*, 649; I read authors from the North and others from the South.) He recalls the fashionable genres of his time: comedy, tragedy, and d'Urfé's pastoral novel, which has enjoyed enduring success. Historiography is about to come into its own: this is an allusion to his friends Boileau and Racine, named historiographers of the king in 1677. Great lyrical poetry disappeared with the death of Malherbe and Racan. Fittingly, in an epistle addressed to a prelate, the poet concludes with Christian thoughts: he will reform his life and sing the praise of God.

The last important publication of La Fontaine was what is placed today under the title of book 12 of the *Fables*. It is a heterogeneous collection of the poet's work composed during his last years, containing not only fables but *contes* and poems. Some of these were published previously in 1685 in the *Ouvrages de prose et de poésie des sieurs de Maucroix et de La Fontaine* and in the *Mercure galant* in 1690 and 1691. Philip A. Wadsworth has given an excellent analysis of this "uneven" book of the twilight years, which, however, contains some outstanding, eloquent fables, "Le Philosophe scythe," already published in 1685, and "Le Juge arbitre, l'hospitalier et le solitaire," the closing fable of the collection.[6]

This volume came out in September 1693, with the date of 1694, under the title *Fables choisies*. It was published by Barbin and dedicated to the duc de Bourgogne, son of the Grand Dauphin to whom La Fontaine had dedicated the 1668 *Fables,* and grandson of Louis XIV. The young duc de Bourgogne was born in 1682; his tutor, Fénelon (1651–1715) gave to his pupil fables of La Fontaine to develop in Latin and later wrote his famous novel *Télémaque* (1699) to educate him in his kingly duties. The novel has mythological characters and setting, disguising political and social realities of the seventeenth century. La Fontaine used a similar setting in "Les

Compagnons d'Ulysse"; however, rather than with political ideas, it deals with philosophical ones and seems to be a follow-up to the first "Discours à Madame de La Sablière."

The dedicatory epistle to the duc de Bourgogne opening the volume is written in the encomiastic style required on such occasions when addressing a prince of royal blood, heir to the throne of France. La Fontaine praises the child's intelligence and sound judgment, in literary matters as well as in other fields. As suggested by Wadsworth, La Fontaine probably meant to add the aesopic fables of 1693 to those of 1668, dedicated to the father of the duc de Bourgogne.[7] He mentions Aesop in the epistle and attributes to these fables a useful, didactic purpose: "Les Animaux sont les précepteurs des Hommes dans mon Ouvrage . . . vous voyez mieux que moi le profit qu'on en peut tirer." (*Fables*, 316; Animals instruct men in my work . . . you see better than I do the profit that can be drawn from them.) The volume contains commissioned pieces, requested for the pleasure or instruction of the prince, such as "Le Loup et le renard," "Le Chat et les deux moineaux," "Les Deux Chèvres" and "Le vieux chat et la jeune souris."

The first fable, "Les Compagnons d'Ulysse," is dedicated to the duc de Bourgogne. It deals with a well-known mythological subject: the myth of the sorceress Circe in Homer's *Odyssey* (10. 135–399). The notion that Ulysses' companions would prefer their animal condition to their human one appears later in Plutarch's *Moralia,* an important book in the Renaissance, mentioned by Rabelais as required reading for Pantagruel (*Pantagruel,* chap. 8, letter of Gargantua to his son Pantagruel) and translated in French by Amyot in 1572. Couton mentions Italian versions of the Circe legend (*Fables,* 535, n. 1), especially Machiavelli's whose works La Fontaine knew since he had used some of them for his *Contes.* The editor also notes an opera by Thomas Corneille and de Visé, *Circé,* performed in 1674.

In the prologue, La Fontaine again praises the young prince's intelligence and the military victories of the prince's father, the Grand Dauphin. His duty performed, he presents Plutarch's version of the legend: Circe has changed the Greeks into various animals by giving them a magic potion. In Homer, they were changed into swine. In La Fontaine a humorous reversal prevents the story from taking a tragic turn: Circe falls in love with Ulysses who obtains from her the promise that she will return his companions to their human form. But they all refuse to return to their previous condition, claiming to be satisfied with the new one. The lion is delighted with his new power and does not want to return to the condition of a private in the army or of a simple citizen in Ithaca. The bear does not think his physique repulsive: female bears find him attractive and he enjoys freedom and happiness. The wolf, accused of eating sheep, retorts that men eat them too; moreover they are cruel to each other according to Hobbes's phrase *homo homini lupus*. All of them prefer the freedom of the woods, a simple, primitive life in which they can follow their instincts and satisfy their desires. None of them believe in heroic deeds nor in the reputation attached to them. The lesson drawn for the benefit of the prince is the traditional view of the moralists: people believe they are free when they obey their passions, but they are in fact enslaved by them.

Wadsworth has judiciously emphasized the contrast between the conventional lesson at the end, the epic style used to recount Ulysses' adventures, and the humorous tone of the sentimental episode showing Circe falling in love with the Greek warrior. He also sees in this fable many of the themes close to La Fontaine's heart: freedom, love, pleasure, similarity of nature between humans and animals. The accusation of bestiality made by the wolf against human beings recalls the "misanthropic fables of 1678–79," "L'homme et la couleuvre" and "Le Loup et les bergers."[8] We have mentioned human bestiality and cruelty as a recurrent motif in other fables as well. Because of this ambivalent attitude, the critic speculates that the poet may have written an earlier version of the fable; when in 1690, a text for the duc de Bourgogne was needed, he could have added the encomiastic prologue and the edifying moral that contradicts the cynical views of the fable proper.[9] This hypothesis seems quite plausible.

It receives support from the very incisive reading of the fable by Richard Danner who points out its disturbing ambiguities.[10] The critic shows that in fact, far from being a heroic, glorious adventure, the sea voyage represents for Ulysses' companions a series of hardships and misfortunes: they are therefore perfectly justified in choosing to remain in their new condition. Metamorphosis has been very beneficial to them. Their arguments are so sound that Ulysses cannot respond to them: "The most fitting candidate for the impartial reader's amused *censure* is Ulysses, who proves to be no match for the articulate beasts whose new life is incomparably nicer than their former state."[11]

Again we see a relativist point of view: Ulysses, from an anthropocentric stance, considers the bear ugly. The metamorphosed bear replies that in bear terms, he is judged handsome.[12] The implicit Lafontainian amused comment is: do not judge others by your own standards, there are several kinds of beauty and happiness in the world, all harmonized with the individual or the species' needs. Of course, for the royal child, he had to present something of a less philosophical nature, hence the moral as it now stands. To the modern reader the moral seems something of a mismatch with the ironic but sensible choice of the companions.

In any event, the fable certainly debunks heroic myths and philosophical and theological assumptions of human superiority over the rest of creation. According to these traditional views, humans possess the faculty of reasoning, but "the non-human debaters in 'Les Compagnons d'Ulysse' are endowed with keen forensic skill."[13] They show judgment and will in the amusing refrain "Je ne veux point changer d'état." Through their experience of both conditions, human and animal, they have discovered the most advantageous and the most pleasurable; perhaps they have discovered themselves: "One can plausibly contend that the repeated refusal of change . . . springs from a profound *connaissance de soi* and is grounded in the poem's internal logic: for these creatures, it is far better to be a quadruped who enjoys living than to be a pitiful, wind-blown human being for whom life, reduced to the hardships of perpetual travel, is an ordeal to be endured."[14] The critic finds the narrative and aesthetic elements superior to the substance of the moral statements. The narrative here is both entertaining with its tongue-in-cheek humor and thought-provoking in its debunking of human arrogance: the received notion of human superiority through reason is implicitly questioned.

The preference for a free and pleasurable life expressed by the metamorphosed companions of Ulysses corresponds to basic human instinct or inclination: in "Le Philosophe scythe," La Fontaine says clearly that it should not be suppressed, but intelligently directed. He probably felt that the free play of instincts should not bring humans to the level of pure and simple animality but be cultivated in a humanistic way. We have argued elsewhere that the metaphor of the garden allows him to examine the relationship between nature and culture. In this fable the garden represents a combination of both, offering beauty and happiness to its owner, a wise man described in hyperbolic terms:

> Homme égalant les Rois, homme approchant des Dieux,
> Et, comme ces derniers satisfait et tranquille.
> Son bonheur consistait aux beautés d'un Jardin.
>   ("Le Philosophe scythe," 12, 20, *Fables,* 348)

> A sage . . .
> Who seemed a king or god, remote from mundane things,
> Since like the gods he was at peace and all seemed well.
> Now a garden enabled his life to expand.
>   ("The Scythian Philosopher," 12, 20, p. 305)

His work as a gardener consists of pruning his trees to make them more productive: intelligent, rational cultivation improves on nature.[15] But the Scythian philosopher does not see the difference between selective pruning and chopping off branches indiscriminately. One must remember that in the ancient world Scythians were considered a nation of barbarians. Far from being an enlightened and wise person, as his title of philosopher would seem to imply, the Scythian shows himself ignorant and thoughtless: he tries to imitate without first learning gardening skills; he destroys everything, not only on his property but by giving bad advice to his neighbors, on their properties also, by lack of knowledge and judgment. He ignores the natural laws of weather, season, and moon cycles, and thus creates havoc. The lesson applies to the psychological and moral realm. Prudently, La Fontaine attributes to the Stoic the unfortunate and unwise attitude of attempting to suppress all human desires and passions. He may have been thinking of all rigorist positions that bring death to the human heart and soul.

> Contre de telles gens, quant à moi, je réclame.
> Ils ôtent à nos coeurs le principal ressort;
> Ils font cesser de vivre avant que l'on soit mort.
>   (12, 20, *Fables,* 349)

> (As for me, such perverted logic is my bane.
> Don't smother the fire in my heart which makes life dear;
> Do not snuff me out yet. I'm not laid on my bier.
>   12, 20, p. 306)

This shows confidence in nature and reason combined. Human intelligence, properly trained by observation to understand the laws of nature, can put them to good use and improve on them. Again, we see the poet as a modern, experimental, and rationalist thinker.

"Le Renard anglais," appropriately dedicated to Madame Harvey, an esteemed English friend, widow and sister of English ambassadors, shows again intelligence and reasoning in an animal, a fox pursued by dogs. Like Madame de La Sablière, the lady refuses to be praised. La Fontaine had several French friends exiled in England: in particular Saint-Evremond and Hortense Mancini, duchesse de Mazarin, who had a circle of admirers; the duchesse de Bouillon had joined them in 1687 (*Fables,* 548–49, n. 3 and 20). Thus England represented already in the seventeenth century—it will more and more do so in the eighteenth century—freedom, personal and intellectual:

> Les Anglais pensent profondément;
> Leur esprit, en cela, suit leur tempérament.
> Creusant dans les sujets, et forts d'expériences,
> Ils étendent partout l'empire des Sciences.
> ("Le Renard anglais," 12, 23, *Fables,* 352)

> (The English mind is a thorough one,
> Effecting what temperament urges be done,
> Pursuing things to their source with tireless diligence,
> Till the sciences expand in consequence.
> "The English Fox," 12, 23, p. 309)

La Fontaine had praised in "Un Animal dans la lune" (7, 17) the interest shown by the English, including the king, Charles II, for sciences based on experimentation. The admiration for an enlightened country and its humane, likable monarch who prefers love to praise, is obvious: La Fontaine thought of joining his friends there. The mention of Madame de Mazarin, who through her charm has made of England "l'Ile de Cythère" (the island of Venus), ends this delightful fable on a note of *galanterie,* especially suitable for the ladies.

Book 12 contains not only fables but poems and *contes,* first published in 1682 with "Le Quinquina." We have mentioned *"Belphégor"* in Chapter 3 and *"La Matrone d'Ephèse"* while discussing the fable "La Jeune Veuve" in Chapter 4. The poems are the charming "Daphnis et Alcimadure," an imitation of Theocritus, as indicated by La Fontaine himself. It is an idyll, set in ancient Greece with shepherds as protagonists; it is dedicated to the second daughter of Madame de La Sablière, a widow, Madame de La Mésangère: was the poem intended to encourage her to remarry? It may well be so, since La Fontaine considered shared love the basis for happiness.

We mentioned briefly "Philémon et Baucis," inspired by Ovid's *Metamorphoses*, in Chapter 1, as possibly a wistful meditation of the poet on lasting conjugal love, which he did not realize in his own marriage, and in Chapter 2 as a replica of *Adonis*. At the end of his career, it orchestrates again, in a different mode, the simple, but essential happiness of shared love in a bucolic setting. Here, moreover, that love is blessed by the gods. The poem is dedicated to the duc de Vendôme, a descendant of Henri IV and his famous favorite, Gabrielle d'Estrées. It was fitting to dedicate a love poem to the descendant of a king named "le Vert-Galant." It also illustrates the patronage that the Vendômes gave to La Fontaine in his later years. The duke and his brother, "le Grand Prieur," were the sons of the duc de Mercoeur and Laure Mancini, another niece of Mazarin and sister to the duchesse de Bouillon. They were in disfavor at court and had a circle of freethinking, fun-loving friends who enjoyed wild parties in Paris at the residence of the Grand Prieur, "le Temple," and at the château of Anet, a lovely setting in the country west of Paris. It had been built in the Renaissance for another royal favorite, Diane de Poitiers. The epilogue of "Philémon et Baucis" is a long encomiastic passage addressed to the duc de Vendôme, praising his "virtues": he was a military man, known for his bravery, his taste for literature, and for establishing the château d'Anet as a shelter for Apollo and the Muses.

The last fable, "Le Juge arbitre, l'hospitalier et le solitaire," is quite controversial, as far as the date of its composition and its religious meaning are concerned.[16] It was published for the first time in June 1693 by the Jesuit Bouhours, in a collection of poems, *Recueil de vers choisis* (*Fables*, 556). The source is again Arnauld d'Andilly's *Vies des saints pères du désert*, which La Fontaine had used for his "Saint Malc." In the fable, the first two saints choose an active religious life; one as an unpaid judge, the second taking care of the sick in a hospital. They receive only complaints in return for their services. They seek the third saint, who is retired in a solitary spot, near a spring surrounded by rocks. He advises them to find a solution to their problems in themselves:

> Apprendre à se connaître est le premier des soins
> Qu'impose à tous mortels la Majesté suprême.
> ("Le Juge arbitre, l'hospitalier et le solitaire,"
> 12, 24, *Fables,* 389)

> (Ask yourself and thus take the best course that you can.
> I think the Almighty would have it our foremost aim.
> "The Judge, the Hospitaler, and the Hermit," 12, 24,
> p. 311.)

As an illustration, he stirs the water of the pool: the visitors cannot see themselves. When the sediments are allowed to settle, they can see their reflection in the water. The agitation of the world prevents people from seeing themselves in a clear mirror.

The lesson seems to be a general one, recapturing the ancient wisdom of "know thyself." It is connected to the lyrical meditation on solitude in the second part of "Le Songe d'un habitant du Mogol" (11, 4). The Christian source of the fable, the term "solitaire," used by men who had chosen a retreat at Port-Royal, La Fontaine's own religious conversion at the time of his illness in February 1693, and Madame de La Sablière's pious exhortations and saintly death in 1693,[17] have led several commentators to attribute to this fable a Christian or even a Jansenist slant. This view has been disputed by other scholars who have pointed out the worldly aspect of the lesson, its Socratic wisdom, its timely advice to courtiers and financiers of seventeenth-century France:[18]

> O vous dont le Public emporte tous les soins,
>   Magistrats, Princes et Ministres,
> Vous que doivent troubler mille accidents sinistres,
> Que le malheur abat, que le bonheur corrompt,
> Vous ne vous voyez point, vous ne voyez personne.
> (12, 24, *Fables,* 389–90)

> (O ministers, judges, and you near the throne,
>   Who deal with the world of fact,
> You are the hampered whom misfortune has attacked,

However powerful, whom good fortune corrupts.
Though you look at friends, it's as if your eyes were gone.

12, 24, p. 312)

Odette de Mourgues sees in the fable an intellectual exercise towards perfection though lucidity.[19] Jean-Pierre Collinet offers a balanced view: the hermit does not so much invite his friends to die to the world and repent their sins as to find themselves, to listen to the inner voice, thus leaning towards wisdom and a philosophical position under apparent submission to Christian dogma: his religion is closer to Socrates' than to Port-Royal.[20] Bernard Beugnot shares de Mourgues's and Collinet's positions.[21] In a study devoted entirely to the last fable, he concludes that the final statement of La Fontaine is not an "élévation," in the spiritual sense of the term (Bossuet wrote some *Elévations sur les mystères*), but the closing of an itinerary, made by the poetic self who is able to reserve in a cruel universe a small, intimate space for his dreams. Under the cover of an edifying tale, borrowed from the Greek fathers, appears an individual dedicated to a profane solitude.[22] Of course, La Fontaine's spiritual itinerary is not recounted in a single fable, by definition a fiction; it was a private matter. But this does not mean that a Providential vision is absent from the *Fables;* on the contrary, we have indicated its presence as a recurring theme. Religious feeling existed in the poet's personality from his early years with the short-lived novitiate at the Oratoire. It comes through in the works, even in the *Contes,* as noted by Henri Busson,[23] but if he was throughout his life a sincere believer, La Fontaine was also a very broad-minded one.

Chapter Eight
Conclusion

Reading this study, the student of La Fontaine can realize firsthand the variety of the poet's literary production, the catholicity of his taste and interests. Far from being only the celebrated author of the *Fables,* he tried his hand at many genres. He was certainly faithful to his motto: "Diversité, c'est ma devise." He started his literary career with an attempt at comedy. Unsure of himself, he decided to adapt one by a well-known Latin playwright, Terence, and wrote *L'Eunuque.* The lack of success of this first attempt did not discourage him, and he soon discovered his true vocation, perhaps listening to some majestic and well-crafted lines by Malherbe. But his genius did not inspire him to follow in the footsteps of Malherbe.

He discovered his true poetic temperament with his first masterpiece, *Adonis.* It blossomed in the enchanted circle of Vaux, among congenial fellow writers and artists, appreciative admirers and a generous patron, Fouquet. In *Adonis,* he drew inspiration not only from its source, Ovid's *Metamorphoses,* but also from a number of genres: it is a "poème héroïque" which is also an idyll, a tragedy, an elegy, and ends as a hymn. The blending of these various genres and styles is already remarkable; the fusion is perfected in the *Fables.* Obviously, La Fontaine enjoyed cultivating the various poetic forms at his disposal and artfully bringing them together in a literary creation that is not a patchwork, but has an internal coherence, be it a long poem or a relatively short fable.

This is, precisely, his supreme accomplishment within the limited framework of the fable. Traditionally a didactic genre, in the hands of La Fontaine it is completely transformed in its inner substance and style, although he does make use of the format handed down to him through several cultures and over many centuries. He respects his masters, the ancients and some modern writers, but with true originality and charming modesty sets out to do something else, to open a new path to Parnassus. He is truly a subversive writer, an iconoclast. While stating, in mock-heroic style, that he is simply revamping aesopic characters, he is making fun of himself as a failed epic poet: "Je chante les Héros dont Esope est le Père. . . ." ("A Monseigneur le Dauphin," *Fables,* 31; I sing when Aesop's wand animates my lyre. "To His Royal Highness the Dauphin," p. 11) He is, in fact, creating a new fictional world, an "ample comédie à cent actes divers / Et dont la scène est l'univers," well before Balzac's *Comédie humaine,* and, at the same time, a new form, since, as Wadsworth judiciously remarks, "like every true artist, he was obliged to create his own medium."[1] Concern with that new form is a welcome addition to the body of La Fontaine scholarship.[2]

He was genuinely interested in new ideas, admiring both Descartes and Gassendi, and thrilled with the new discoveries of his time, thus he can be considered a modernist; he did not miss an opportunity to denounce and make fun of superstitious beliefs and practices,[3] and thought that experimental verifications and rational thinking were necessary at every step in the process of acquiring new knowledge. But, while a thinking man, he was not a philosopher, rather a poet who made some humorous remarks on human weaknesses and who candidly admits that he shares in them. He was a dreamer, not in the common, derogatory sense of the term, but a man living in another world, "toujours beau, toujours divers, toujours nouveau": the reverie, the daydreams are, for him, creative. He becomes inspired by a beautiful setting,—whether projected through a dream as in *Le Songe de Vaux*—or actual, as Versailles in *Psyché* and Anet in the later years, which probably contributed to the bucolic charm of "Philémon and Baucis." But the dreams were translated into poetry "dreamlike yet full of concrete observation of mankind, pungently humorous, yet tinged with melancholy, amusingly personal yet endowed with the wisdom of the ages. . . . The springlike freshness of his poetry, as of his personality, stayed with him all his life and has remained unforgettably alive across the centuries."[4]

Notes and References

The following abbreviations have been used throughout for the titles of journals:

CAIEF   *Cahiers de l'association internationale des études françaises*
F.R.   *French Review*
PFSCL   *Papers on French Seventeenth Century Literature*
RHLF   *Revue d'histoire littéraire de la France*

Chapter One

1. Georges Mongrédien, *Recueil des textes et des documents du XVIIe siècle relatifs à La Fontaine* (Paris: Centre national de la recherche scientifique, 1973); hereafter cited as *Recueil*.

2. François de Dainville, "Collèges," in *Dictionnaire des lettres françaises, XVIIe siècle.* (Paris: Fayard, 1954).

3. Abbé d'Olivet, *Histoire de l'académie française 1792*, ed. Charles L. Livet, 2 vols. (Paris: Didier, 1858), 2: 303. Philip Wadsworth, in his *Young La Fontaine* (Evanston, Ill.: Northwestern University Press, 1952), 4, cautions the reader: d'Olivet "was not always well informed." Further references to Wadsworth follow in the text.

4. Lucian, Greek sophist and satirist, second century A.D. His language is considered fairly easy, suitable for second or third year students of Greek.

5. On the teaching of Greek in seventeenth-century France, see R. C. Knight, *Racine et la Grèce* (Paris: Nizet, 1974), chap. 2, "L'Enseignement du grec au XVIIe siècle"; chap. 3, "Les Formes de l'hellénisme au XVIIe siècle". On secondary education in France in the sixteenth and early seventeenth century, see George Huppert, *Public Schools in Renaissance France* (Urbana and Chicago: University of Illinois Press, 1984), chap. 12. The author traces the turnover of the municipal tuition-free "collèges" to Jesuit teachers under Henri IV and Richelieu, who were interested in bringing "independent secondary schools under the tutelage of the central government." For a thorough treatment of the "collèges" in the seventeenth century, the role of the Jesuits in education, the setting up of their *Ratio studiorum*, and the stress on teaching classical authors and rhetoric, see Roger Chartier, Dominique Julia, and Marie-Madeleine Compère, *L'Education en France du XVIe au XVIII siècle* (Paris: SEDES, 1976), chap. 5 and 6.

6. La Fontaine, "Epître à Monseigneur l'Evêque de Soissons," referred to by modern scholars as the "Epître à Huet," in *Oeuvres diverses,*

ed. Pierre Clarac, (Paris: Gallimard, Pléiade, 1958), 648; in *Oeuvres complètes*, ed. Jean Marmier (Paris: Seuil, 1965), 493. Further references to these editions follow in the text.

7. Noémi Hepp, *Homère en France au XVIIe siècle* (Paris: Klincksieck, 1968), 76.

8. Ibid, 489–90, especially n. 119.

9. Knight, *Racine et la Grèce*, 21, quotes Rollins's *Traité des études* (1, 82) and discusses the various approaches to the teaching of Greek, showing the superiority of the Port-Royal method in obtaining fluency. The author states that no one in the first generation of classical writers claimed a knowledge of Greek, 38–39. He quotes the testimonies of Louis Racine and d'Olivet concerning La Fontaine but notes that the latter took the side of the "anciens" in the famous "Querelle des Anciens et des Modernes."

10. The Prince de Condé (1621–86) was born Louis de Bourbon, duke of Enghien. He was raised in the Jesuit collège of Bourges and had an excellent education. He befriended and protected the major writers of the period. He was well known for his military skills, had a brilliant career as a general, starting at twenty-two with the victory of Rocroi in 1643.

11. Pierre Clarac, *La Fontaine par lui-même* (Paris: Seuil, 1961), 11–12.

12. Antoine Furetière (1619–88), scholar, novelist. Author of a dictionary, published in Holland in 1690. Since the French Academy considered his undertaking as disloyal competition to their own *dictionnaire*, he was excluded in 1685.

13. Mongrédien, *Recueil*, 40.

14. Ibid., 207.

15. Philippe Sellier, *Pascal et Saint Augustin* (Paris: A. Colin, 1970), 11, states that "The 17th century is St. Augustine's century." The basic text of Jansenist theology is Jansenius *Augustinus* (1640), a commentary on Augustine's doctrines.

16. Wadsworth, *Young La Fontaine*, 37–44, on the influence of Ovid and other classical poets. See also his "Ovid and La Fontaine," *Yale French Studies* 38 (1967): 153; Jean-Pierre Collinet, *Le Monde littéraire de la Fontaine* (Paris: P. U. F., 1970), 10–11; Madeleine Defrenne, "Le Phénomène créateur chez La Fontaine: le poète et le monde," *Australian Journal of French Studies* 12 (1975): 126; Jean Marmier, *Horace en France au XVIIe siècle* (Paris: P. U. F., 1962), chap. 9, "La Fontaine et Horace," 311–39.

17. Jean-Pierre Chauveau, "La Poésie du siècle baroque," in Jean-Charles Payen et Jean-Pierre Chauveau, *La Poésie des origines à 1715* (Paris: A. Colin, 1968), 175–76. The author suggests that the master who might have spoiled his style may be Théophile.

18. Abbé d'Olivet, *Histoire de l'académie française*, 2:303–4, in Mongrédien, *Recueil*, 36.

19. Philip A. Wadsworth, "La Fontaine as Student and Critic of Malherbe," *Symposium* 3 (May 1949): 130–39.

20. Marc Fumaroli, "Les Enchantements de l'éloquence: *Les Fées* de Charles Perrault ou De la littérature," in *Le Statut de la littérature, Mélanges offerts à Paul Bénichou* (Geneva: Droz, 1982), 156–59. The author mentions the first *Fables* of La Fontaine.

21. Born and raised as a protestant, Pellisson was first noticed by Fouquet and remained loyal to him after the latter's arrest. He spent several years in prison at the Bastille. Released through the efforts of his devoted friend Madeleine de Scudéry, he gained the favor of Louis XIV who offered him the position of royal historiographer provided he would convert to catholicism. Pellisson started to write a *History of the French Academy,* which gave him access to that prestigious body.

22. Philip A. Wadsworth, "La Fontaine and His views on Marriage," *Rice University Studies,* 51, no. 3 (Summer 1965): 81–96.

23. Tallemant des Réaux, "Racan et autres resveurs," in *Historiettes* (1657), ed. Antoine Adam (Paris: Gallimard, Pléiade, 1960), 1: 391–92.

24. Wadsworth, "La Fontaine and Marriage," 82.

25. Le Limousin, a province in the center of France, the major city and capital of which is Limoges.

Chapter Two

1. Tallemant, *Historiettes,* 1: 1054, n. 1.

2. Orest Ranum, *Artisans of Glory. Writers and Historical Thought in 17th Century France* (Chapel Hill: University of North Carolina Press, 1980), 244–45; Wadsworth, *Young La Fontaine,* 17.

3. Marc Fumaroli, Introduction to *France in the Golden Age* by Pierre Rosenberg (New York: The Metropolitan Museum of Art, 1982), 16.

4. The Fronde was the civil war that took place between 1648 and 1652. The government of the regent queen, Anne of Austria, and her minister, Cardinal Mazarin, was opposed by the old feudal aristocracy on one hand and by the magistrates of the *parlement* on the other. For a recent update on the political aspects of Fouquet's career, see Daniel Dessert, "L'Affaire Fouquet," *L'Histoire,* 32 (mars 1981): 39–47. On his patronage, Urbain-Victor Chatelain, *Le Surintendant Nicolas Fouquet, protecteur des lettres, des arts et des sciences* (1905; reprint ed., Geneva: Slatkine Reprints, 1971); Wolfgang Leiner, "Nicolas Foucquet au jeu des miroirs," *Cahiers de l'association internationale des études françaises,* 22 (mai 1970): 249–75; J-P. Collinet, "La Fontaine et Foucquet" in *L'Age d'or du Mécénat 1598–1661* (Paris: Centre national de la recherche scientifique, 1985), 273–82.

5. Ranum, *Artisans,* 148.

6. Alain Niderst, *Madeleine de Scudéry, Paul Pellisson et leur monde* (Paris: P. U. F., 1976), 356–57, 394.

7. Leiner, "Nicolas Foucquet," 270.

8. Paul Valéry, "Au sujet d'Adonis," in *Oeuvres,* ed. Jean Hytier (Paris: Gallimard, Pléiade, 1957), 474–95.

9. J-P. Collinet, *Le Monde littéraire de La Fontaine* (Paris: P. U. F., 1970), 41.

10. Madame de Sévigné, *Correspondance,* ed. Roger Duchêne, 3 vols. (Paris: Gallimard, Pléiade, 1972), vol. 1, letters 59 and 65, quotes Fouquet's words during his trial stressing his loyalty to the king.

11. Jean Rousset, *"Psyché* ou le plaisir des larmes," in *L'Intérieur et l'Extérieur* (Paris: Corti, 1968), 115.

12. See Sévigné, *Correspondance,* 1: 48–82.

13. Nicole Ferrier-Caverivière, *L'Image de Louis XIV dans la littérature française de 1660 à 1715* (Paris: P. U. F., 1981), 133–34, 175, 187.

14. On royal jealousy see Madeleine Bertaud, *La Jalousie dans la littérature française au temps de Louix XIII* (Geneva: Droz, 1981), 23–36.

15. Renée Kohn, *Le Goût de La Fontaine* (Paris: P. U. F., 1962), 94.

16. Bernard Beugnot, "l'Idée de retraite dans l'oeuvre de La Fontaine," *CAIEF,* 26 (mai 1974): 136.

17. G. Guisan, "L'Evolution de l'art de La Fontaine d'après les variantes de l'*Adonis,*" *RHLF* 42 (1935): 161–80 and 321–43.

18. John C. Lapp, "Ronsard and La Fontaine. Two versions of *Adonis,*" *L'Esprit créateur,* 10, no. 2 (Summer 1970): 136.

19. Jacqueline Van Baelen, "La Chasse d'Adonis," *L'Esprit créateur,* 21, no. 4 (Winter 1981): 23.

20. All quotations in English translation of La Fontaine's *Fables* are from Marianne Moore, *The Fables of la Fontaine* (New York: Viking, 1954).

21. Pascal, *Pensées,* ed. Philippe Sellier (Paris: Mercure de France, 1976), 97–98.

22. Jean Lafond, "Augustinisme et épicurisme au XVIIe siècle," *XVIIe Siècle* 34, no. 2 (avril-juin 1983): 149.

23. Collinet, *Le Monde littéraire,* 50.

24. *Ibid.,* 49.

25. Willian Calin, *"Militia* and *Amor:* A Reading of *Adonis,*" *L'Esprit créateur* 21, no. 4 (Winter 1981): 28–40; Collinet, *Le Monde littéraire.* 46–50; Marie-Odile Sweetser, *"Adonis,* poème d'amour: conventions et création poétiques," *L'Esprit créateur* 21, no. 4 (Winter 1981): 41–49.

26. Madeleine Defrenne, "Le Traitement du lieu commun dans l'*Adonis* de La Fontaine," *Revue des langues vivantes* 42 (1976): 258–77.

27. Ronsard, *Adonis,* in *Oeuvres complètes,* ed. Gustave Cohen (Paris: Gallimard, Pléiade, 1938), 2:25–33; Shakespeare, *Venus and Adonis,* in *The Complete Plays and Poems of William Shakespeare,* The New Cambridge Edition (Cambridge, Mass.: Houghton Mifflin, 1942), 1333–46.

28. Wadsworth, *Young La Fontaine,* 37–44; Collinet, *Le Monde littéraire,* 11; Madeleine Defrenne, "Le Phénomène créateur," 126.

29. David Lee Rubin, *Higher, Hidden Order: Design and Meaning in the Odes of Malherbe,* University of North Carolina Studies in Romance Languages and Literatures, no. 117 (Chapel Hill: University of North Carolina Press, 1972), 112.

30. Robert E. Hallowell, *Ronsard and the Conventional Roman Elegy,* Illinois Studies in Languages and Literature, vol. 37, no. 4 (Urbana: University of Illinois Press, 1954), 26–29, 37–46.

31. See n. 17.

32. See n. 18.

33. Collinet, *Le Monde littéraire,* 50.

34. Jean-Michel Pelous, *Amour précieux, amour galant 1654–1675* (Paris: Klincksieck, 1980), 32.

35. Van Baelen, "La Chasse d'Adonis," 23.

36. Marie-Odile Sweetser, "La Femme abandonnée: esquisse d'une typologie," *PFSCL,* 10 (1978–79): 168.

37. See n. 21.

38. Collinet, *Le Monde littéraire,* 41–42; Valéry, "Au sujet d'*Adonis,*" 488–91.

39. Ibid., 492–93.

40. Erwin Panowsky, "*Et in Arcadia ego.* Poussin et la tradition élégiaque," in *L'Oeuvre d'art et ses significations. Essais sur les arts visuels* (Paris: Gallimard, 1969), 284.

41. Jean de La Fontaine, *Le Songe de Vaux,* ed. illustrée avec introduction, commentaires et notes par Eleanor Titcomb, Textes littéraires français (Geneva: Droz, 1967), 29–30.

42. "Where will I not climb up?" See Jean Orieux, *La Fontaine ou la vie est un conte* (Paris: Flammarion, 1976), 186.

43. Titcomb, Introduction to *Le Songe,* 73–74.

44. Ibid., 41, 77, 80.

45. On the waters, see William Roberts, "The Claims of Hortésie in *Le Songe de Vaux,*" in *Voyages. Récits et Imaginaire. Actes de Montréal,* ed. Bernard Beugnot, *Biblio 17,* no. 11 (Paris, Seattle, Tubingen: PFSCL, 1984), 316–36.

46. *Le Songe,* 119, nn. 58 and 59.

47. Robert Nicolich, "The Triumph of Language: The Sister Arts and Creative Activity in La Fontaine's *Songe de Vaux*", *L'Esprit créateur* 21, no. 4 (Winter 1984): 10–21.

48. *Le Songe,* 138.

49. Roberts, "The Claims of Hortésie," 323.

50. Collinet, *Le Monde littéraire,* 102–3.

51. Louis Roche, *La Vie de Jean de La Fontaine* (Paris: Plon, 1913), 159, quoted by Clarac, *O.D.,* 900.

52. Clarac, *O.D.*, 902.

53. Ibid., 903.

54. J-P. Collinet, Madeleine Defrenne, and Yvonne Champigneul, *Le Voyage de La Fontaine dans le Limousin* in *La Découverte de la France au XVIIe siècle* (Paris: Centre national de la recherche scientifique, 1980), 43–63; See also Madeleine Defrenne, "Le Stéréotype du voyage et son utilisation poétique et narrative dans l'oeuvre de La Fontaine" in *Voyages. Récits et Imaginaire*, 275–92.

Chapter Three

1. Georges Couton, Introduction to *Contes et Nouvelles en vers*, by La Fontaine (Paris: Garnier, 1961), x–xi.

2. Mongrédien, *Recueil*, 42.

3. Couton, Introduction, xii.

4. Pelous, *Amour précieux*, passim.

5. Couton, Introduction, xvi–xvii; Nicole Ferrier et Jean-Pierre Collinet, Introduction to *Contes et Nouvelles en vers*, by La Fontaine (Paris: Garnier-Flammarion, 1980), 17. All quotations of the *Contes* refer to this edition, hereafter cited as *Contes*.

6. Valéry, "Au sujet d'*Adonis*," 493–94.

7. Couton, Introduction, i–ii.

8. John C. Lapp, "The Esthetics of Negligence: La Fontaine's *Contes*," *L'Esprit créateur* 3 (1963): 108–15; rpt. in *Une Fenêtre ouverte sur la création. Essais sur la littérature française*, ed. Cynthia B. Kerr (Tübingen: Gunter Narr; Paris: J-M. Place, 1983), 64.

9. John C. Lapp, *The Esthetics of Negligence: La Fontaine's "Contes"* (New York: Cambridge University Press, 1971), 1–2.

10. Ibid., 77.

11. J-P Collinet, "La Fontaine et l'Italie" in *L'Italianisme en France, Studi francesi*, Supplement to 35 (Maggio-Agosto 1968) (Torino: Societá editrice internazionale, 1968), 119–24.

12. Ferrier et Collinet, Introduction, 24.

13. Ibid., 18.

14. *Dissertation sur la Joconde*, texte établi et présenté par Charles-H. Boudhors, in *Oeuvres complètes de Boileau* (Paris: Les Belles Lettres, 1966), 22; the editor believes Nicolas Boileau-Despréaux was the author of the *Dissertation*, 127–34; Antoine Adam, *Histoire de la littérature française au XVIIe siècle*, 5 vols. (Paris: Domat, 1952), 3: 83–85; Pierre Clarac, *Boileau* (Paris: Hatier, 1964), 48–57, believe that Gilles Boileau wrote most of it, probably with the help of his younger brother, Nicolas Boileau-Despréaux; Jules Brody, *Boileau and Longinus* (Geneva: Droz, 1958), 27–28 attributes it to Boileau; Constant Venesoen, "Un problème de paternité: Qui a écrit la *Dissertation sur Joconde?*", *XVIIe Siècle* 88 (1970): 31–48,

reviews previous arguments by major Boileau scholars and concludes in favor of La Fontaine himself; Bernard Beugnot et Roger Zuber, *Boileau, Visages anciens, visages modernes* (Montréal: Presses de l'université de Montréal, 1973), 99–100 give a concise and useful summary of the question.

15. See Jane Merino-Morais, *Différences et répétition dans les "Contes" de La Fontaine* (Gainesville: University of Florida Press, 1981), 24–26, for onomastic comments.

16. Couton, Introduction, xxiii; Ferrier et Collinet, Introduction, 19–20.

17. Pierre Clarac, Introduction to *Contes et Nouvelles en vers*, by La Fontaine (Paris: Les Belles Lettres, 1961), xviii.

18. Collinet, *Le Monde littéraire*, 287.

19. See Henri-Jean Martin, *Livres, pouvoirs et société à Paris au XVIIe siècle (1598–1701)*, (Genève: Droz, 1969), 2 vol. II, 754 and 593 about Gaspard Migeot of Mons, "Migeon" was a misspelling.

20. Couton, Introduction, xxvi–xxvii.

21. Jean-Pierre Collinet, "La matière et l'art du prologue dans les *Contes* de La Fontaine," *Studi francesi*, 74 (Maggio-Agosto, 1981), 219–37.

22. Defrenne, "Stéréotype," 275–92.

23. Jane Merino-Morais, *Différence et répétition*.

24. Lapp, *The Esthetics of Negligence*, 159. See chap. 6, "Poetic Techniques."

Chapter Four

1. Nicole Boursier, "La Loi et la règle," *Papers on French Seventeenth Century Literature*, 10, no. 19 (1983): 651–71.

2. Wadsworth, *Young La Fontaine*, 211.

3. Simone Blavier-Paquot, *La Fontaine: Vues sur l'art du moraliste dans les fables de 1668* (Paris: Les Belles Lettres, 1961), 11.

4. Wadsworth, *Young La Fontaine*, 211.

5. Pierre Boutang, *La Fontaine politique* (Paris: J-E. Hallier-Albin Michel, 1981), 31.

6. Couton, Introduction, iv.

7. On the fable in medieval literature, see Urban T. Holmes, *A History of Old French Literature from the Origins to 1300* (New York: Crofts & Co., 1938), 207–20.

8. Wadsworth, *Young La Fontaine*, 179.

9. Olivier Patru, *Lettres à Olinde* in *Oeuvres diverses*, 2 vol. (Geneva: Slatkine Reprints, 1972), 2: 411–23.

10. Wadsworth, *Young La Fontaine*, 179.

11. Couton, Introduction, vii–viii.

12. Ibid., xiv–xv.

13. Ibid., xv; J-P. Collinet, Preface to *Satires, Epitres, Art poétique,* by Nicolas Boileau, Collection Poésie (Paris: Gallimard, 1985), 24.

14. G. Couton, Introduction, xvii.

15. Jean Marmier, *Horace en France au 17e siècle* (Paris: P. U. F., 1962), chap. 9, "La Fontaine et Horace," 311–39; On Horace and Terence, see H. Gaston Hall, "*Contaminatio* in a fable by La Fontaine (I, 3)," *PFSCL,* 11 (1979): 91–106; Ph. Wadsworth, "Ovid and La Fontaine," *Yale French Studies* 32 (May 1967): 151–55.

16. Robert Aulotte, *Mathurin Régnier. Les Satires* (Paris: SEDES, 1983), 63–64.

17. J-P. Collinet, Introduction to the *Fables,* 12–14.

18. M. de Périgny at his death in 1670 was replaced by Bossuet.

19. Ferrier-Caverivière, *L'Image de Louis XIV,* 19, 47, 60, 134.

20. Susan W. Tiefenbrun, "Signs of Irony in La Fontaine's *Fables*": *PFSCL,* 11 (1979): 51–76; rpt. in *Signs of the Hidden. Semiotic Studies* (Amsterdam: Rodopi, 1980), 143.

21. Jacques-Henri Périvier, "La Cigale et la fourmi' comme introduction aux *Fables,*" *French Review,* 42, no. 3 (February 1969): 423.

22. Ibid., 421

23. Marcel Gutwirth, "Réflexions sur le métier de poète: trois fables de La Fontaine," in *Le Statut de la littérature. Mélanges offerts à Paul Bénichou,* ed. Marc Fumaroli (Geneva: Droz, 1982), 137–42.

24. David Lee Rubin, "Four Modes of Double Irony in La Fontaine's *Fables,*" in *The Equilibrium of Wit. Essays for Odette de Mourgues,* ed. Peter Bayley and Dorothy Gabe Coleman (Lexington, Ky.: French Forum, 1982), 207.

25. Ibid., 208.

26. Ibid., 205–6.

27. Richard Danner, "Individualism in *Le Loup et le chien,*" *Kentucky Romance Quarterly* 24, no. 2 (1977): 186–87, 189; Richard Danner, *Patterns of Irony in the Fables of La Fontaine* (Athens: Ohio University Press, 1985), 73–74, 83.

28. Jules Brody, "Irony in La Fontaine: from Message to Massage," *PFSCL* 11 (1979): 81.

29. Ibid., 84–85.

30. Susan Tiefenbrun, "The Art and Artistry of Teaching in the *Fables* of La Fontaine," *L'Esprit créateur,* 21, no. 4 (Winter 1981): 50–65.

31. June Moravcevich, "Reason and Rhetoric in the *Fables* of La Fontaine," *Australian Journal of French Studies,* 16, no. 3 and 4 (1979): 355–56.

32. René Jasinski, *La Fontaine et le premier recueil des fables* 2 vols. (Paris: Nizet, 1966), 1: 244–48; Marc Soriano, "Fantasme et complexe d'Oedipe à l'époque de Louis XIV. Problèmes de méthode et premiers résultats des recherches concernant La Fontaine," *PFSCL,* no 10, 2, *Actes de*

Toronto (1978–79): 177–84, gives a psychoanalytical reading of "Le Loup et l'agneau" and "La Grenouille qui veut se faire aussi grosse que le boeuf."

33. Raymond LePage, "The 1668 Edition of the *Fables:* An Iconographic Interpretation," *L'Esprit créateur,* 21, no. 4 (Winter 1981): 69.

34. Marcel Gutwirth, "Réflexions sur le métier de poète," 143–45.

35. Odette de Mourgues, *O Muse, fuyante proie* (Paris: Corti, 1962). 169–76; Marcel Gutwirth, *"Le Chêne et le roseau* ou les cheminements de la mimesis," *F.R.,* 48, no. 4 (March 1975): 695–702.

36. Rubin, "Four Modes," 202.

37. Hepp, *Homère en France,* 471.

38. Rubin, "Four Modes," 203.

39. Ibid., 204.

40. Danner, *Patterns of Irony,* 96–100.

41. Georges Couton, *La Politique de La Fontaine* (Paris: Les Belles Lettres, 1959), 54–56.

42. Jasinski, *La Fontaine et le premier recueil,* 2: 16–17.

43. Couton, *La Politique,* 56.

44. Ibid., 57–59; André Georges, "La Pensée politique de Cinna," *Romanic Review,* 74, no. 4 (November 1983): 413–24.

45. Jacqueline Duchêne, *Françoise de Grignan ou le mal d'amour* (Paris: Fayard, 1985), 16–17.

46. Jasinski, *La Fontaine et le premier recueil,* 2: 85.

47. Danner, *Patterns of Irony,* 100–4.

48. Jasinski, *La Fontaine et le premier recueil,* 2: 186–87.

49. Collinet, *Le Monde littéraire,* 173.

50. Jasinski, *La Fontaine et le premier recueil,* 2: 202, indicates a parody of Virgil's *Aneid* in this description.

51. Richard Danner, "Selection and Sacrifice in La Fontaine's *Le Satyre et le Passant,*" *PFSCL,* 8 (1977–78): 195–207.

52. Jasinski, *La Fontaine et le premier recueil,* 2: 283–84.

53. See *XVIIe Siècle,* 131 (avril-juin 1981), *Antiquité chrétienne et antiquité païenne dans la culture française du XVIIe siècle,* especially Marc Fumaroli, *Avant-propos,* and Roger Zuber, "Guez de Balzac et les deux antiquités."

54. Danner, *Patterns of Irony,* 56–57.

55. Ibid., 58.

56. Jean-Dominique Biard, *The Style of La Fontaine's Fables* (Oxford: Blackwell, 1968), 180. Quoted by Danner, *Patterns of Irony,* 59.

57. Danner, *Patterns of Irony,* 60.

58. J-P. Collinet, "L'Image de la femme dans les *Fables* de La Fontaine," in *Onze nouvelles études sur l'image de la femme dans la littérature française du 17e siècle,* ed. Wolfgang Leiner, Etudes littéraires françaises, no. 25 (Tübingen: Gunter Narr; Paris: J-M Place, 1984), 134.

59. J-D. Biard, *The Style*, 13–14.

60. Collinet, *Le Monde littéraire*, 231–33.

Chapter Five

1. Kohn, *Le Goût de La Fontaine*, 115.

2. Ibid., 116.

3. Lucius Apuleius, Platonic philosopher and rhetorician, born in Numidia, a Roman province in Africa, about 125 A.D. His main work is the *Metamorphoses* or *The Golden Ass*, which contains marvelous tales.

4. Rousset, "*Psyché* ou le plaisir des larmes," 116.

5. Wadsworth, *Young La Fontaine*, 116–17; see also Clarac, *La Fontaine*, 90–91.

6. For an excellent update on the question, see Beugnot et Zuber, *Boileau*, 110–11.

7. Rousset, "*Psyché* ou le plaisir des larmes," 117–18.

8. Collinet, *Le Monde littéraire*, 266–67. See also the preface to *Satires*, by Nicolas Boileau (Paris: Gallimard, 1985), 19–20, 26.

9. Marie-Odile Sweetser, "Le Jardin: Nature et culture chez La Fontaine," *CAIEF* 34 (Mai 1982): 59–72.

10. Clarac, *La Fontaine*, 90.

11 Ibid., 93; Mongrédien, *Recueil*, 95, 96–97.

12. This grotto was taken down in 1684 to make room for the construction of the north wing of the château, *O.D.*, 827, n. 5.

13. The importance of love and jealousy in the novels of the first half of the seventeenth century has been well studied by Bertaud, *La Jalousie*, 234–70.

14. The question of readers' response has been studied by Joan DeJean, "La Fontaine's *Psyché:* The Reflecting Pool of Classicism," *L'Esprit créateur* 21, no. 4 (Winter 1981): 99–109; also Nathan Gross, "Functions of the Framework in La Fontaine's *Psyché*," *PMLA* 84 (May 1969): 583–84.

15. Jacques Barchilon, "Wit and Humor in La Fontaine's *Psyché*," *F.R.* 26 (1962): 23–31.

16. Pelous, *Amour précieux*, 154, quotes *Psyché* as one of the most important examples of "littérature galante" and states that its charm is made of contrasting and alternating between emotion and jest.

17. Noémi Hepp, "De l'amour galant à l'amour sublime: l'envol de Psyché, *Cahiers de littérature du XVIIe siècle* 6 (1984): 239–46.

18. Jacqueline Van Baelen, "*Psyché:* vers une esthétique de la liberté" in *La Cohérence intérieure. Etudes sur la littérature française du XVIIe siècle présentées en hommage à Judd D. Hubert* (Paris: J-M Place, 1977), 177–86, mentions "une structure binaire," 178.

19. Sweetser, "Le Jardin," 67: "La Fontaine belongs to Descartes' century, even though he was on the side of the Ancients in literature."

20. Barchilon, "Wit and Humor," 23–31.

21. Margaret McGowan, "La Fontaine's Techniques of Withdrawal in *Les Amours de Psyché et de Cupidon*," *French Studies* 18 (1964): 322–31.

22. John L. Logan, "The Poetics of Preterition in *Les Amours de Psyché*," *PFSCL* 4/5 (Summer 1976): 11–28.

23. John L. Logan, "*Psyché:* A Critical Study" (Ph.D. diss., Yale University, 1975), 243.

24. Gross, "Functions of the Framework," 586.

25. Rousset, "*Psyché* ou le plaisir des larmes," 115–24.

26. Jules Brody, "Pierre Nicole auteur de la préface du *Recueil de poésies chrétiennes et diverses*," *XVIIe Siècle* 64 (1964): 31–54.

27. Jean Lafond, "La Beauté et la Grâce. L'esthétique platonicienne des *Amours de Psyché*," *RHLF* 69, no. 3-4 (mai-août 1969): 475–90.

28. Collinet, *Le Monde littéraire*, 268–83.

29. Van Baelen, "*Psyché:* vers une esthétique de la liberté," 177–86.

30. De Jean, "La Fontaine's *Psyché*," 99–109.

31. Michael Vincent, "Voice and Text: Representation of Reading in La Fontaine's *Psyché*," *F.R.* 57, no. 2 (December 1983): 179–86.

32. Hepp, "De l'amour galant à l'amour sublime," 239–46.

33. See n. 26.

34. The father of the young prince, Armand de Conti, a libertine in his youth and one time protector of Molière in Languedoc in the 1650s, and his mother, Anne-Marie Martinozzi, niece of Mazarin, had both converted to an austere religious life.

35. Wadsworth, *Young La Fontaine*, 107, sees "an undercurrent of humor" in the first *élégie*, but not in the others.

36. Donna Kuizenga, "The Language of Love: La Fontaine's *Elégies pour Clymène*," *PFSCL* no 13, 1/2 (1980): 25–40, argues that the *Elégies* are based on reversal, "capable-incapable" in the first; "esclave-monarque" in the second; "L'Amant se meurt" in the third and "amour-amitié" in the fourth.

37. Collinet, *Le Monde littéraire*, 293–94.

38. Madame de La Sablière (1640–93), born Marguerite Hessein in a wealthy protestant family of bankers, married Antoine de Rambouillet, sieur de La Sablière from whom she separated in 1668. Well educated, she read Latin and Greek and was interested in science. She received in her town house a brilliant and freethinking group, among them the doctor and philosopher François Bernier, a great traveler and popularizer of Gassendi's Epicurean doctrine. Abandoned by her faithless lover, the marquis de La Fare, she converted to Catholicism and retired to the Hospice des Incurables, a hospital for terminally ill patients, to devote herself to charity work.

Chapter Six

1. Clarac, *La Fontaine,* 99–100.
2. Collinet, *Le Monde littéraire,* 314–24.
3. See Bernard Beugnot's masterful essay, "Autour d'un texte: L'ultime leçon des *Fables,*" in *Mélanges Pintard, Travaux de linguistique et de littérature,* no. 13, pt. 2 (Strasbourg: Centre de philologie et de littérature romanes de l'université de Strasbourg, 1975), 291–301.
4. Collinet, *Le Monde littéraire,* 341.
5. Ibid., 344–45; Hepp, *Homère en France,* 489–94.
6. Collinet, *Le Monde littéraire,* 335.
7. Couton, *Fables,* 465, n. 3.
8. Leo Spitzer, "The Art of Transition in La Fontaine," in *Essays on Seventeenth-Century French Literature,* ed. and trans. Davis Bellos (New York: Cambridge University Press, 1983), 183; Patrick Dandrey, "L'Emergence du naturel dans les *Fables* de La Fontaine. A propos du *Héron* et de *La Fille,*" RHLF 83, no. 3 (mai-juin 1983): 378–79.
9. Collinet, *Le Monde littéraire,* 205–6.
10. J-P. Collinet, "La Fontaine, *La Fille* et la Grande Mademoiselle," in *Mélanges Couton* (Lyon: Presses Universitaires de Lyon, 1981), 359–71.
11. Spitzer, "The Art of Transition," 181–83.
12. Danner, *Patterns of Irony,* 55.
13. Spitzer, "The Art of Transition," 197.
14. G. Couton, "Le Livre épicurien des *Fables:* Essai de lecture du livre VIII," in *Mélanges Pintard,* 283–90.
15. Ibid, 284–85.
16. Henriette-Marie de France (1609–66), sister of Louis XIII had married Charles I (1600–49) of England in 1625. Their children were Charles II (1630–85) and Henriette-Anne, Madame (1644–70), married to Philippe d'Orléans (1640–1701), brother of Louis XIV (1638–1715).
17. Louis Marin, *Le Récit est un piège* (Paris: Edition de Minuit, 1978), 19.
18. De Mourgues, *O Muse, fuyante proie,* 177–82; Alain Seznec, "Connaissance philosophique-creation poétique: Discours à Madame de la Sablière," in *The Equilibrium of Wit.*
19. Michael Vincent, "Transtextual Traps: *Le Rat et l'huître,*" PFSCL, 12, no. 22 (1985): 42.
20. J-P. Collinet, "*Du Rat domestique et l'Ouytre* anonyme au *Rat et l'huître* de La Fontaine," PFSCL 12, no. 22 (1985): 59–67.
21. Danner, *Patterns of Irony,* 70–71.
22. Spitzer, "The Art of Transition," 193–94.
23. Michael Vincent, "Fragmented Lovers Discourse: Textuality and Sexuality in La Fontaine's *Les Deux Pigeons,*" PFSCL 9, no. 17 (1982): 675–90.

24. Ibid., 680–81.

25. René Jasinski, "Sur la philosophie de La Fontaine dans les livres VII à XII des *Fables*," *Revue d'Histoire de la philosophie* 1 (1933): 316–31; 2 (1934): 218–41.

26. H. Busson and F. Gohin, Introduction to *Discours à Madame de La Sablière (Sur l'âme des animaux)* by La Fontaine, Textes Littéraires Français (Geneva: Droz, 1967), 9–41.

27. Ibid., 16.

28. Ibid., 101–5. The text of Nicolas Denys on the beavers is reproduced in the appendix.

29. Ibid., 28; Beverly Ridgely, "Beavers, Bobacks and Owls: Reality and Fantasy in Three Episodes of Animal Behavior in the *Fables* of La Fontaine," *PSFCL,* 4/5 (1976): 39–40.

30. Ridgely, "Beavers, Bobacks," 41–44.

31. Busson, Introduction, 38.

32. Alain Seznec, "Connaissance philosophique—création poétique: *Discours à Mme de La Sablière*" in *The Equilibrium of Wit,* 223.

33. Ibid., 224–26.

34. Ibid., 217

35. Danner, *Patterns of Irony,* 152–54.

36. Henri Lafay, "*L'Homme et la couleuvre* ou la parole de La Fontaine: Analyse de fonctionnement textuel," in *Mélanges Couton,* 373–82.

37. Richard Danner, "La Fontaine's *Fables,* Book X: The Labyrinth Hypothesis," "*L'Esprit créateur* 21 no. 4 (Winter 1981): 90–98; Danner, *Patterns of Irony,* 149.

38. Ibid., 154, 159–60; Rubin, *Higher, Hidden Order: Design and Meaning in the Odes of Malherbe,* 20–21.

39. Roger Zuber, "*Le Songe d'un habitant du Mogol:* Etude littéraire," *Bulletin de la faculté des lettres de l'université de Strasbourg* 41 (1963): 361–70.

40. Couton, *La Politique de La Fontaine,* 92–95.

41. Marcel Gutwirth, "*Le Paysan du Danube,* Dialogue à trois voix: Guevara, La Fontaine, Hippolyte Taine," in *Mélanges Couton,* 383–91.

Chapter Seven

1. Clarac, *La Fontaine,* 127; see also Beverly Ridgely, "Disciple de Lucrèce une seconde fois: A Study of La Fontaine's *Poéme du quinquina,*" *L'Esprit créateur,* 11, no. 2 (Summer 1971): 92–122.

2. Boileau, Bernier, Molière, et al., *L'Arrêt burlesque* (1671), in *Oeuvres complètes de Boileau,* ed. Charles-H. Boudhors (Paris: Les Belles Lettres, 1966), 31–35, 140–42.

3. Mongrédien, *Recueil,* 201.

4. Ibid., 134–35.

5. Collinet, *Le Monde littéraire*, 391.

6. Philip A. Wadsworth, "Le Douzième Livre des *Fables*," *CAIEF* 26 (Mai 1974): 103–15.

7. Ibid., 106.

8. Ibid., 108–9.

9. Ibid., 110.

10. Richard Danner, "La Fontaine's *Compagnons d'Ulysse:* The Merits of Metamorphosis," *F.R.*, 53, no. 2 (December 1980): 239–47.

11. Ibid., 242.

12. Ibid.: "Humans may have the right to set standards of human beauty, but they are not thereby entitled to evaluate the beauty or ugliness of bears."

13. Ibid., 245.

14. Ibid., 246.

15. Sweetser, "Le Jardin," 65–67.

16. Wadsworth, "Le Douzième Livre," 111.

17. Léon Petit, *La Fontaine à la rencontre de Dieu* (Paris, Nizet, 1970) 135–51.

18. Wadsworth, "Le Douzième Livre," 112, 115.

19. De Mourgues, *O Muse, fuyante proie*, 99.

20. Collinet, *Le Monde littéraire*, 409.

21. Bernard Beugnot, "L'Idée de retraite dans l'oeuvre de La Fontaine," *CAIEF* 26 (Mai 1974): 141.

22. Bernard Beugnot, "Autour d'un texte: l'ultime leçon des *Fables*," in *Mélanges Pintard*, 291–301.

23. Henri Busson, *La Religion des classiques* (Paris: P. U. F., 1948), chap. 10, "Le confrère Jean de La Fontaine," 292–97.

Chapter Eight

1. Wadsworth, *Young La Fontaine*, 219.

2. David L. Rubin, "A Genre Renewed: Formal Reflections on the *Fables*," *PFSCL*, 10, no. 19 (1983): 747–55. Other young scholars are working in that direction, Richard Danner, Susan Tiefenbrun, and Michael Vincent among them.

3. Beverly S. Ridgely, "Astrology and Astronomy in the *Fables* of La Fontaine," *PMLA* 80 (1965): 180–89.

4. Wadsworth, *Young La Fontaine*, 219–20.

Selected Bibliography

PRIMARY SOURCES

1. French

Editions *Oeuvres,* Edited by Henri Régnier. 11 vols. Paris: GELF, Hachette, 1883–97.

Oeuvres complètes. 2 vols. Paris: Gallimard, Pléiade. Vol. 1, *Fables, contes et nouvelles,* edited by Edmond Pilon, René Groos, and Jacques Schiffrin, 1954; Vol. 2, *Oeuvres diverses,* edited by Pierre Clarac, 1958. Outstanding editions.

Oeuvres complètes. Paris: Seuil, 1965. Preface by Pierre Clarac. Edited by Jean Marmier. Chronologie.

Contes et nouvelles en vers. Edited by Pierre Clarac. Paris: Les Belles Lettres, 1934.

Contes et nouvelles en vers. Edited by Georges Couton. Paris: Garnier, 1961.

Contes et nouvelles en vers. Edited by Nicole Ferrier et Jean-Pierre Collinet. Paris: Garnier Flammarion, 1980.

Discours à Mme de La Sablière (sur l'âme des animaux). Edited by H. Busson et F. Gohin. Textes Littéraires Français. Geneva: Droz, 1967.

Fables choisies mises en vers. Edited by Georges Paris: Couton. Garnier, 1962.

Fables. Edited by Jean-Pierre Collinet. Collection Poésie/Gallimard. 2 vols. Paris: Gallimard, 1974.

Fables. Edited by Marc Fumaroli. Illustrated by Marie Hugo. 2 vol. Paris, Imprimerie nationale, 1985. Handsome new edition with stimulating introduction.

Le Songe de Vaux. Edited by Eleanor Titcomb. Textes Littéraires Français. Geneva-Paris: Droz-Minard, 1967.

2. Translations

A Hundred Fables of la Fontaine. With pictures by Percy J. Billinghurst. New York: Greenwich House, 1983.

Boone, Bruce, and Robert Gluck, trans. *La Fontaine.* San Francisco: Black Star Series, 1981. Translations of fables, letters, *contes.*

Cairncross, John. trans. *La Fontaine Fables and Other Poems.* Gerards Cross, England: Colin Smythe, 1982. Thirteen fables of La Fontaine.

Moore, Marianne, trans. *The Fables of La Fontaine.* New York: Viking Press, 1954.

James Michie, trans. *Selected Fables*. Introduction by Geoffrey Grigson.
New York: Viking Press, 1979.
C.H. Sisson, trans. *Some Tales of La Fontaine*. Introduction by Sisson.
Manchester, England: Carcant, 1979.

SECONDARY SOURCES

1. Bibliographies

Beugnot, Bernard, and J-M. Moureaux, *Manuel bibliographique des études
littéraires. Les bases de l'histoire littéraire. Les voies nouvelles de l'analyse
critique*. Paris: Nathan, 1982.
Cabeen, David C., and Jules Brody. *A Critical Bibliography of French
Literature*. Syracuse, N.Y.: Syracuse University Press. Vol. 3, *The
Seventeenth Century*, edited by Nathan Edelman, 1961. Chapter 2:
Poetry, Section on La Fontaine by Arthur Whittem and Philip A.
Wadsworth, 114–24; Vol. 3A, *The Seventeenth Century*, Supplement,
edited by Gaston Hall, 1983. Chapter 2: Poetry, section on La Fontaine by Philip A. Wadsworth, 87–97. Excellent. Highly recommended for critical comments by a major La Fontaine scholar.
Cioranescu, Alexandre. *Bibliographie de la littérature française du dix-septième
siècle*. 3 vols. Paris: Centre National de la recherche scientifique,
1965–66.
*French 17. An Annual Descriptive Bibliography of French Seventeenth Century
Studies*. Edited by J. D. Vedvik. Published for the Seventeenth Century French Division of the Modern Language Association of America
by Colorado State University, Fort Collins, Colorado. Most recent
issue, 1985.
Klapp, Otto. *Bibliographie d'histoire littéraire française*. Frankfurt: Kloster-
mann, 1956–.
Rancoeur, René. *Bibliographie de la littérature française du moyen âge à nos
jours*. Paris: A. Colin, 1967. Appearing in *RHLF* issues under *Bibliographie*, divided by century.
Van Baelen, Jacqueline. *La Fontaine: Répertoire bibliographique de la critique
1955–1975*, in *PFSCL* 7 (Summer 1977): 121–63.

2. Dictionaries

Cayrou, Gaston. *Le Français classique. Lexique de la langue du XVIIe siècle*.
Paris: Didier, 1948.
Dubois, Jean, René Lagane, and Alain Lerond. *Dictionnaire du français
classique*. Paris: Larousse, 1971.
Grente, Cardinal Georges. *Dictionnaire des lettres françaises. Le Dix-septième
siècle*. Paris: Arthème Fayard, 1954.

3. Background Material

Adam, Antoine. *Histoire de la littérature française au XVIIe siècle.* Vol. 4, chap. 1. Paris: Domat, 1954.

Busson, Henri. *La Religion des classiques,* 271–97. Paris: P. U. F., 1948.

Chartier, Roger, Dominique Julia, and Marie-Madeleine Compère, *L'éducation en France du XVIe au XVIIIe siècle.* Paris: SEDES, 1976.

Duchêne, Jacqueline, *Françoise de Grignan ou le mal d'amour.* Paris: Fayard, 1985.

Ferrier-Caverivière, Nicole. *L'Image de Louis XIV dans la littérature française de 1660 à 1715.* Paris, P.U.F., 1981. Many references to La Fontaine's works.

Fumaroli, Marc. "Des leurres qui persuadent les yeux," Introduction *France in the Golden Age. Seventeenth Century French Paintings in American Collections,* by Pierre Rosenberg. New York: Metropolitan Museum of Art, 1982.

——"Les enchantements de l'éloquence: les *Fées* de Charles Perrault ou De la littérature", in *Le Statut de la littérature. Mélanges offerts à Paul Bénichou,* edited by Marc Fumaroli. Genève: Droz, 1982, 153–186.

Goubert, Pierre. *Louis XIV et vingt millions de français.* Paris: Fayard, 1966; *Louis XIV and Twenty Million Frenchmen.* Translated by Anne Carter. New York: Pantheon, 1970.

Hepp, Noémi. *Homère en France au XVIIe siècle.* Paris: Klincksieck, 1968.

Huppert, George. *Public Schools in Renaissance France.* Urbana and Chicago: University of Illinois Press, 1984.

Marmier, Jean. *Horace en France au 17e siècle.* Publications de la faculté des lettres et sciences humaines de Rennes. Paris: P. U. F., 1962.

Martin, Henri-Jean. *Livres, pouvoirs et société à Paris au XVIIe siècle (1598–1701).* Genève: Droz, 1969, 2 vol.

Mousnier, Roland. *Les Institutions de la France sous la monarchie absolue 1598–1789.* 2 vols. Paris: P. U. F., 1974, 1980.

Niderst, Alain. *Madeleine de Scudéry, Paul Pellisson et leur monde.* Paris: P. U. F., 1976.

Payen, Jean-Charles, and Jean-Pierre Chauveau. *La Poésie des origines à 1715.* Collection U. Paris: A. Colin, 1968. "L'Epoque de Louis XIV" by J-P. Chauveau, 178–201, includes a section on La Fontaine, 184–93.

Pelous, Jean-Michel. *Amour précieux, amour galant (1654–1675). Essai sur la représentation de l'amour dans la littérature et la société mondaines.* Paris: Klincksieck, 1980.

Ranum, Orest. *Artisans of Glory. Writers and Historical Thought in seventeenth century France.* Chapel Hill: University of North Carolina Press, 1980.

Tocanne, Bernard. *L'Idéee de nature en France dans la seconde moitié du 17e siècle. Contribution à l'histoire de la pensée classique.* Paris: Klincksieck, 1978.

Van Delft, Louis. *Le Moraliste classique. Essai de définition et de typologie.* Histoire des idées et critique littéraire, vol. 202. Geneva: Droz, 1982. Many excellent considerations on La Fontaine.

Wolf, John B. *Louis XIV.* New York: W. W. Norton, 1968.

Zuber, Roger, avec **Micheline Cuénin.** *Littérature française* Collection Littérature française/Poche, dirigée par Claude Pichois. Paris: Arthaud, 1984. Vol. 4, *Le Classicisme 1660–1680.* Chapter 12, "La Fontaine," by M. Cuénin. An outstanding introduction to the poet, and summation.

————"Atticisme et classicisme" in *Critique et création littéraires en France au XVIIe siècle.* Paris: CNRS, 1977, 375–87.

4. La Fontaine Studies in Collective volumes and Reviews

L'Age d'or du Mécénat 1598–1661. Actes du colloque international du centre national de la recherche scientifique (mars 1983) réunis et publiés par Roland Mousnier et Jean Mesnard. Paris: Centre national de la recherche scientifique, 1985.

Cahiers de l'association internationale des études françaises, no. 26 (mai 1974). Section on La Fontaine.

La Découverte de la France au XVIIe siècle. Colloques internationaux du Centre national de la recherche scientifique. Paris: Centre national de la recherche scientifique, 1980. "Le Voyage de La Fontaine dans le Limousin": articles by J-P. Collinet, M. Defrenne, and Y. Champigneul, 43–63.

The Equilibrium of Wit: Essays for Odette de Mourgues. Edited by Peter Bayley and Dorothy Gabe Coleman. Lexington, Ky.: French Forum, 1982.

L'Esprit créateur 21, no. 4 (Winter 1981). Issue on Jean de La Fontaine. Guest editor David Lee Rubin.

Europe 50 (janv.-mars 1972). Special issue on La Fontaine.

Mélanges Couton, 323–91. Lyon: Presses Universitaires de Lyon, 1981. Articles on La Fontaine by J. Jehasse, R. Dubuis, J-P. Collinet, H. Lafay, and M. Gutwirth.

PFSCL 4/5 (Summer 1976): 7–74. Trois études sur La Fontaine. Introduction by J. Van Baelen. Articles by J. L. Logan, Beverly S. Ridgely, and Philip A. Wadsworth.

PFSCL 11 (1979). Section on La Fontaine. Introduction by J. L. Logan. Articles by Louis Marin, Roseann Runte, Susan Tiefenbrun, Jules Brody, H. Gaston Hall, and Jane Merino.

PFSCL 12, no. 22 (1985). "On Birds and Fables." Articles by H. G. Hall, M. Belcher, M. Vincent and J-P. Collinet.

Voyages. Récits et Imaginaire. Actes de Montréal. Edited by Bernard Beugnot. Biblio 17, no 11. Paris-Seattle-Tübingen: PFSCL, 1984. Part 4, *Autour de La Fontaine,* 273–349. Introduction by Ronald Tobin. Articles by Madeleine Defrenne, Leonard Marsh, and William Roberts. Com-

mentaires par Roseann Runte and Louis Van Delft; G. Donald Jackson
and Michael Vincent; H. Gaston Hall.

5. Critical Studies

Barchilon, Jacques. "Wit and Humor in *Psyché,*" *French Review* 36 (1962): 23–31.

Beugnot, Bernard, and Roger Zuber. *Boileau. Visages anciens, visages nouveaux 1665–1970.* Montréal: Presses de l'université de Montréal, 1973.

Beugnot, Bernard. "L'Idée de retraite dans l'oeuvre de La Fontaine," *CAIEF* 26 (Mai 1974): 131–42.

————. "Autour d'un texte: L'ultime leçon des Fables." In *Mélanges Pintard, Travaux de linguistique et de littérature* 13, part 2. Strasbourg: Centre de philologie et de littérature romanes de l'université de Strasbourg, 1975: 291–301.

————. "Spécularités classiques." In *Destins et enjeux du XVIIe siècle.* Textes réunis par Y-M. Bercé, J-L. Gautier, et Ph. Sellier, 173–81. Paris, P. U. F., 1985.

Biard, Jean-Dominique. *The Style of La Fontaine's Fables.* Oxford: Blackwell, 1966.

————. Introduction to *Vignettes des Fables de La Fontaine* (1668), de François Chauveau. Exeter, England: University of Exeter Press, 1977.

Blavier-Paquot, Simone. *La Fontaine. Vues sur l'art du moraliste dans les Fables de 1668.* Paris: Les Belles Lettres, 1961.

Boursier, Nicole. "La Loi et la Règle," *PFSCL* 10, no. 19 (1983): 651–71.

Bray, Bernard. "Avatars et fonctions du je dans les *Fables* de La Fontaine," in *Mélanges Pintard* 303–22.

Brody, Jules. *Boileau and Longinus.* Geneva: Droz, 1958.

————. "Pierre Nicole auteur de la préface du *Recueil de poésies chrétiennes et diverses,*" *XVIIe Siècle,* 64 (1964): 31–54.

————. "Irony in La Fontaine: from Message to Massage," *PFSCL* 11, (1979): 77–89.

Calin, William. "*Militia* and *Amor*: A Reading of *Adonis, L'Esprit créateur* 21, no. 4 (Winter 1981): 28–40.

Chauveau, François. *Vignette des Fables de La Fontaine* (1668). Introduction par J-D. Biard. Exeter, England: University of Exeter Press, 1977.

Clarac, Pierre. *La Fontaine.* Rev. ed. Connaissance des Lettres, no. 21. Paris: Hatier, 1959.

————. *La Fontaine par lui-même,* Paris: Seuil, 1963.

Collinet, Jean-Pierre. *Le Monde littéraire de La Fontaine.* Paris: P. U. F., 1970. A Lafontainian summa, combining thorough erudition with taste. For specialists and very advanced students.

————. "La Fontaine et Molière," *CAIEF* 26 (1974): 173–85.

————. "La Fontaine et l'Italie." In *L'Italianisme en France au XVIIe siècle*. Actes du 8ème congrès de la société française de littérature comparée (Grenoble-Chambéry, 26–28 mai 1966). Supplement to *Studi francesi* 35 (maggio-agosto 1968), recueillis et publiés par Giorgio Mirandola. Torino, Italy: Società editrice internazionale, 1968: 119–124.

————. "La Fontaine: *Fables*, livres 7–12" *Information littéraire* 31 (1979): 190. Bibliographie.

————. "La Fontaine est-il poète?," *Oeuvres et critiques* 5, no. 1 (Automne 1980): 51–68. Réception de textes lyriques.

————. "Le Voyage de La Fontaine dans le Limousin. La Découverte de la France." In *La Découverte de la France au XVIIe siècle*, 43–49. Paris: Centre national de recherche scientifique, 1980.

————. "La Fontaine, *La Fille* et la Grande Mademoiselle," dans *Mélanges offerts à Georges Couton*, 359–71. Lyon, Presses Universitaires de Lyon, 1981.

————. "La matière et l'art du prologue dans les *Contes* de La Fontaine." *Studi francesi* 74 (maggio-agosto 1981): 219–37.

————. "La Fontaine: de la mythologie à l'affabulation." In *La Mythologie au XVIIe siècle*, 265–74. IIème Colloque, CMR 17, Archives Communales. Marseille. 1982.

————. "L'Image de la femme dans les *Fables* de La Fontaine." In *Onze nouvelles études sur l'image de la femme dans la littérature française du dix-septième siècle*, réunies par Wolfgang Leiner, 121–44. Tübingen: Gunter Narr Verlag; Paris: Jean-Michel Place, 1984.

————. "La Fontaine et Foucquet." In *L'Age d'or du Mécénat 1598–1661*. Actes du colloque international CNRS (mars 1983), publiés par Roland Mousnier et Jean Mesnard, 273–82. Paris: Centre national de la recherche scientifique, 1985.

————. "Les classiques à l'école." In *Destins et enjeux du XVIIe siècle*. Préface de Jean Mesnard. Textes réunis et publiés par Y-M. Bercé, N. Dufourcq, N. Ferrier-Caverivière, J-L. Gautier, et Ph. Sellier, 223–30. Paris: P. U. F., 1985.

————. "L'Image du roi dans les *Fables* de La Fontaine." In *L'Image du souverain dans les lettres françaises des guerres de religion à la révocation de l'édit de Nantes*, 293–308. Actes et colloques no. 24. Paris: Klinck-sieck, 1985.

Couton, Georges. *La Poétique de La Fontaine*. Paris: P. U. F., 1957.

————. *La Politique de La Fontaine*. Paris: Les Belles Lettres, 1959.

————, ed. *Fables choisies mises en vers*. Paris: Garnier, 1962.

Dandrey, Patrick. "La Fable double de *l'Horoscope:* une poétique implicite de La Fontaine," *XVIIe Siècle* 124 (juillet-sept. 1979): 276–86.

————. "Une révolution discrète: les *Fables* de La Fontaine et l'esthétique de la continuité ornée," *PFSCL* 9, no. 17 (1982): 655–74.

————. "L'émergence du naturel dans les *Fables* de La Fontaine. A propos du Héron et de La Fille' ", *RHLF* 83, no. 3 (mai-juin 1983): 371–89.

————. "Séduction du pouvoir: La Fontaine, le berger, et le roi." *Cahiers de Littérature du XVIIe siècle,* no. 8, "Méthodologies" (1986): 9–23.

Danner, G. Richard. "La Fontaine's Ironic Vision in the *Fables,*" *French Review* 50, no. 4 (March 1977): 562–71.

————. "Individualism in La Fontaine's *Le Loup et le Chien,*" *Kentucky Romance Quarterly* 24, (1977): 185–90.

————. "Selection and Sacrifice in La Fontaine's *Le Satyre et le Passant,*" *PFSCL* 8 (Winter 1977–78): 195–207.

————. "Les Compagnons d'Ulysse," *French Review* 54, no. 2 (Dec. 1980): 239–47.

————. *Patterns of Irony in the Fables of La Fontaine.* Athens: Ohio University Press, 1985. Stimulating new study. Provocative readings of many fables.

Defrenne, Madeleine. "Le phénomène créateur chez La Fontaine: le poéte et le monde," *Australian Journal of French Studies* 12 (1975): 119–67.

————. "Le Traitement du lieu commun dans l'*Adonis* de La Fontaine," *Revue des langues vivantes,* 42 (1976): 258–77.

————. "La Fontaine à la découverte du Limousin et d'un mode d'écriture." In *La Découverte de la France au XVIIe siècle,* 51–58: Colloque international du Centre national de recherche scientifique, no. 590. Paris: Centre national de la recherche scientifique.

————. "Le Stéréotype du voyage et son utilisation poétique dans l'oeuvre de La Fontaine." In *Voyages. Récits et Imaginaire. Actes de Montréal,* edited by Bernard Beugnot. 275–91. *Biblio 17,* no. 11. Paris, Seattle, Tübingen: *PFSCL,* 1984.

————. "Premières créatures Lafontainiennes: une approche de la poétique du personnage dans l'oeuvre de La Fontaine," *PFSCL* 19 (1983): 733–46.

DeJean, Joan. "La Fontaine's *Psyché:* The Reflecting Pool of Classicism," *L'Esprit créateur* 21, no. 4 (Winter 1981): 99–109.

Edwards, Michael. "La Fontaine and the Subversion of Poetry." In *The Equilibrium of Wit. Essays for Odette de Mourgues,* edited by Peter Bayley and Dorothy Gabe Coleman, 193–200. Lexington, Ky.: French Forum, 1983.

Fumaroli, Marc. Introduction to his edition of La Fontaine's *Fables.* Paris: Imprimerie nationale, 1985, 2 vol. I, 11–71.

Gross, Nathan. "Functions of the Framework in La Fontaine's *Psyché,*" *PMLA* 84 (May 1969): 577–86.

————. "Strategy and Meaning in La Fontaine's *Adonis,*" *MLN* 84, no. 4 (May 1969): 605–26. Special French issue.

————. "Order and Theme in La Fontaine's *Fables,* Book VI," *L'Esprit créateur* 21, no. 4 (Winter 1981): 78–89.

Guitton, Margaret. *La Fontaine. Poet and Counterpoet.* New Brunswick, N.J.: Rutgers University Press, 1961.

Gutwirth, Marcel. "Le Chêne et le Roseau ou les cheminements de la mimesis," *French Review* 48 (1975): 695–702.

————. "Réflexions sur le métier de poète, trois fables de La Fontaine." In *Le Statut de la littérature. Mélanges offerts à Paul Bénichou,* edited by M. Fumaroli, 137–51. Geneva: Droz, 1982.

————. "*Le Paysan du Danube,* dialogue à trois voix: Guevara, La Fontaine, Hippolyte Taine." In *Mélanges offerts à Georges Couton,* 383–92. Lyon: Presses Universitaires de Lyon, 1981.

————. "*Fable,*" New Orleans, La.: The Graduate School of Tulane University, 1980, 20 p.

————. *Un merveilleux sans éclat. La Fontaine ou la poésie exilée.* Genève: Droz, 1986.

Haddad, Adnan. *Fables de La Fontaine d'origine orientale.* Paris: SEDES, 1984.

Haig, Sterling. "La Fontaine's *Le Loup et le Chien* as a Pedagogical Instrument," *French Review* 42 (1969): 701–5.

Hall, H. Gaston. "*Contaminatio* in a Fable by La Fontaine (I, 3)," *PFSCL* 11 (1979): 91–106.

————. "On some of the Birds in La Fontaine's *Fables,*" *PFSCL* 12, no. 22 (1985): 15–27; see also Margaret Belcher, "La Fontaine's Birds: Some Comment on Gaston Hall's Paper," 29–38.

Hepp, Noémi. "De l'amour galant à l'amour sublime: l'envol de Psyché," *Cahiers de littérature du XVIIe siècle* 6 (1984): 239–48. Hommage à René Fromilhague. Université de Toulouse—Le Mirail.

Hill, Robert E. "The Poem in the Garden: La Fontaine's *Le Songe de Vaux* as a Gloss." *PFSCL* 13, no. 24 (1986): 207–20.

Hubert, Judd D. "La Fontaine et Pellisson, ou le mystère des deux Acante." *RHLF.* 66 no 2 (avril-juin 1966): 223–37.

Hubert, Renée Riese. "Interprétation figurée des *Fables* de La Fontaine." *Kentucky Romance Quarterly* 14 no 3 (1967): 177–91.

Hytier, Jean. "La Vocation lyrique de La Fontaine," *French Studies* 25 (1971): 136–55.

————. "La poésie de La Fontaine: Légitime défense," *French Studies* 26 (1972): 27–29.

Jasinski, René. *La Fontaine et le premier recueil des Fables.* 2 vols. Paris: A. G. Nizet, 1966.

————. "Sur la philosophie de La Fontaine dans les livres VII à XII des *Fables,*" *Revue d'histoire de la philosophie* 1 (1933): 316–30; 2 (1934): 218–42.

Jeanneret, Michel. "*Psyché* de La Fontaine. La recherche d'un équilibre romanesque." In *The Equilibrium of Wit,* 232–48.

Knight, Roy C. *Racine et la Grèce.* Paris: Nizet, 1974. Part 1, chap. 2,

"L'Enseignement du grec au XVIIe siècle"; Chap. 3, "Les Bornes de l'hellénisme au XVIIe siècle."

Kohn, Renée J. "Réflexions sur l'*Adonis* de La Fontaine," *Romanic Review* 47 (1956): 81–91.

————. *Le Goût de La Fontaine.* Paris: P. U. F., 1962.

————. "La Fontaine et le merveilleux," *CAIEF* 26 (mai 1974): 117–29.

Kuizenga, Donna. "The Language of Love: La Fontaine's *Elégies pour Clymène*," *PFCSL* no. 13, 1/2 (1980): 25–40.

Lafay, Henri, "*L'Homme et la Couleuvre* ou la Parole de La Fontaine. Analyse de fonctionnement textuel." In *Mélanges Couton,* 373–82.

————. "Poésie et médecine au XVIIe siècle. Des Blasons des Fleurs (1614) au *Poème du quinquina* (1682)"*Revue Marseille,* no 95, 4 ème trimestre, 1973, 137–141.

Lafond, Jean. "La Beauté et la Grâce. L'Esthétique platonicienne des *Amours de Psyché,*" *RHLF* 69, no. 3–4 (mai-août 1969): 475–90.

————. "Augustinisme et épicurisme au XVIIe siècle," *XVIIe Siècle* 34, no. 2 (avril-juin 1982): 149–68.

Lapp, John C. "The Esthetics of Negligence: La Fontaine's *Contes,*" *L'Esprit créateur* 3 (1963): 108–15.

————. "Ronsard and La Fontaine: Two Versions of *Adonis,*" *L'Esprit créateur* 10, no. 2 (Summer 1970): 125–44.

————. *The Esthetics of Negligence: La Fontaine's Contes.* Cambridge: Cambridge University Press, 1971.

Leiner, Wolfgang. "Nicolas Foucquet au jeu des miroirs," *CAIEF* 22 (mai 1970): 249–75.

Le Page, Raymond, G. "The 1668 Edition of the *Fables:* An Iconographic Interpretation," *L'Esprit créateur,* 21, no. 4 (Winter 1981): 66–77.

Logan, John L. "The Poetics of Preterition in *Les Amours de Psyché,*" *PFSCL* 4 and 5 (Summer 1976): 11–28.

Lyons, John D. "Author and Reader in the *Fables,*" *French Review* 49, no. 1 (October 1975): 59–97.

Malandain, Pierre. *La Fable et l'Intertexte.* Paris: Les Editeurs français réunis, 1981. Collection Entailles.

Marin, Louis. *Le Récit est un piège.* Paris: Editions de Minuit, 1978.

————. "Le Récit originaire, l'origine du récit, le récit de l'origine," *PFSCL* 11 (1979): 13–28.

————"Les tactiques du renard," in *Le Portrait du roi,* Paris, Editions de minuit, 1981, 117–29.

Marmier, Jean. "La Construction des *Elégies* de La Fontaine." In *Mélanges Pintard,* 275–82.

McGowan, Margaret. "La Fontaine's Technique of Withdrawal in *Les Amours de Psyché et de Cupidon,*" *French Studies* 18 (1964): 322–31.

————. "Moral Intention in the *Fables* of La Fontaine," *Journal of the Warburg & Courtauld Institute* 29 (1966): 264–82.

Merino, Jane. "The Play of Deferred Communication in La Fontaine's *La Confidente sans le savoir*," *PFSCL* 11 (1979): 107–17.

Merino-Morais, Jane. *Différence et répétition dans les Contes de La Fontaine.* University of Florida Humanities Monographs, no. 52. Gainesville: University Press of Florida, 1983.

Molinié, Georges. "Sur l'*Adonis* de La Fontaine," *RHLF* 75, no. 5 (sept-oct 1975): 707–29.

Mongrédien, Georges. *Recueil des textes et documents du XVIIe siècle relatifs à La Fontaine.* Paris: Centre national de la recherche scientifique, 1973.

Moravcevich, June. "Reason and Rhetoric in the *Fables* of La Fontaine," *Australian Journal of French Studies* 16, no. 3 and 4 (1979): 347–60.

Mourgues, Odette de. *0 Muse, fuyante proie . . . Essai sur la poésie de La Fontaine.* Paris: José Corti, 1962. Outstanding.

Nicolich, Robert. "The Triumph of Language: The Sister Arts and Creative Activity in La Fontaine's *Songe de Vaux*," *L'Esprit crétaeur* 21, no. 4 (Winter 1981): 10–21.

Orieux, Jean. *La Fontaine ou la vie est un conte.* Paris: Flammarion, 1976.

Périvier, Jacques-Henri. "*La Cigale et la fourmi* comme introduction aux *Fables*," *French Review* 42, no. 3 (Feb. 1969): 419–27.

Petit, Leon. *La Fontaine à la rencontre de Dieu.* Paris: Nizet, 1970.

Raymond, Marcel. "*Psyché* et l'art de La Fontaine," *Génies de France.* Neuchâtel, Switzerland: La Baconnière, 1942.

Ridgely, Beverly. "Astrology and Astronomy in the *Fables* of La Fontaine," *PMLA* 80 (1965): 180–89.

————. "Disciple de Lucrèce une seconde fois. A Study of La Fontaine's *Poème du Quinquina*," *L'Esprit créateur* 11, no. 2 (Summer 1971): 92–122.

————. "Beavers, Bobacks and Owls: Reality and Fantasy in Three Episodes of Animal Behavior in the *Fables* of La Fontaine," *PFSCL* 4/5 (1976): 29–56.

Riffaterre, Michael. "Sémiotique de la description dans la poésie du dix-septième siècle." In *Actes de Fordham,* ed. Jean Macary. *Biblio* 17, no. 9 (1983): 93–124 (Paris, Seattle, and Tübingen: *PFSCL,* 1983). On *Le Songe de Vaux* and *Psyché,* see 117–20.

Roberts, William. "The Claims of Hortésie in *Le Songe de Vaux*," in *Voyages . . . Actes de Montréal,* 316–36.

Roche, Louis. *La Vie de Jean de La Fontaine.* Paris: Plon-Nourrit, 1913.

Rousset, Jean. "*Psyché* ou le plaisir des larmes." In *L'Intérieur et l'extérieur.* Paris: Corti, 1968.

————. "*Psyché* ou le génie de l'artificiel," In *Renaissance, Maniérisme, Baroque. Actes du XIe stage international de Tours.* Paris: J. Vrin, 1972.

Rubin, David Lee. *Higher, Hidden order: Design and Meaning in the Odes of Malherbe.* University of North Carolina Studies in the Romance Languages and Literatures, no. 117. Chapel Hill: University of North Carolina Press, 1972.

————. ed. "Réception de textes lyriques français. Problèmes, méthodes, perspectives." In *Oeuvres et critiques* 5, no. 1 (Automne 1980): 5–8.

————. Introduction, *L'Esprit créateur* 21, no. 4 (Winter 1981): 7–9. Special issue on La Fontaine edited by Rubin.

————. "Four Modes of Double Irony in La Fontaine's *Fables.*" In *The Equilibrium of Wit,* 201–12.

————. "A Genre Renewed: Formal Reflections on the *Fables* of Jean de La Fontaine," *PFSCL* 10, no. 19 (1983): 747–55.

————. "On Dream in La Fontaine's *Fables,*" *PFSCL* 11, no. 20 (1984): 115–22.

Sévigné, Madame de. *Correspondance.* Edited by Roger Duchêne. 3 vols. Paris: Gallimard, Pléiade, 1972-1978.

Seznec, Alain. "Connaissance philosophique—création poétique: *Discours à Mme de la Sablière.*" In *The Equilibrium of Wit,* 213–31.

Shaw, David. "La Fontaine's Letters to His Wife," *Modern Languages* (1972): 125–35.

————. "L'Esthétique de la structure dans *Psyché* de La Fontaine," *Studi francesi,* 49 (gennaio-aprile 1973): 15–27.

Soriano, Marc. "Histoire littéraire et folklore. La source oubliée de deux fables de la Fontaine," *RHLF* 70 (1970): 836–60.

————. "Des *Contes* aux *Fables,*" *Europe* 515 (1972): 99–131.

————. "Fantasme et complexe d'Oedipe à l'époque de Louis XIV. Problèmes de méthode et premiers résultats de recherches concernant La Fontaine," *PFSCL* 10, no. 2 (1978–79): 177–94. *Actes de Toronto.*

Spitzer, Leo. "The Art of Transition in La Fontaine." In *Essays on 17th Century French Literature.* Translated, edited, and with an introduction by David Bellos. Cambridge: Cambridge University Press, 1983.

Sweetser, Marie-Odile. "*Adonis,* poème d'amour. Conventions et création poétiques," *L'Esprit créateur,* 21, no. 4 (Winter 1981): 41–49.

————. "Le Jardin: Nature et culture chez La Fontaine," *CAIEF* 34 (Mai 1982): 59–72.

————. "Le mécénat de Fouquet: la période de Vaux et ses prolongements dans l'oeuvre de La Fontaine." In *L'Age d'or du Mécénat 1598–1661,* 263–72. Paris: Centre national de la recherche scientifique, 1985. Actes du colloque international du centre national de la recherche scientifique Mousnier-Mesnard.

Tiefenbrun, Susan W. "Signs of Irony in La Fontaine's *Fables,*" *PFSCL* 11 (1979): 51–76. Reprint in *Signs of the Hidden. Semiotic studies.* Amsterdam: Rodopi, 1980.

————. "The Art and Artistry of Teaching in the *Fables* of La Fontaine," *L'Esprit créateur* 21, no. 4 (Winter 1981): 50–65.

Titcomb, Eleanor. Introduction to *Le Songe de Vaux,* by La Fontaine, 1–49. Geneva: Droz, 1967.

Turk, Edward Baron. "La Fontaine: mythologue et mythologicien," *French Literature Series* 3 (1976): 28–37.

Tyler, J. Allen. *A Concordance to the Fables and Tales of Jean de La Fontaine.* Edited by J. Allen Tyler. Ithaca: Cornell University Press, 1974.

Van Baelen, Jacqueline. Introduction to "Trois Etudes sur La Fontaine," *PFSCL* 4 and 5 (Summer 1976): 7–9.

————. "*Psyché:* vers une esthétique de la liberté." In *La Cohérence intérieure. Etudes sur la littérature française du XVIIe siècle* présentées en hommage à Judd D. Hubert, 177–86. Paris: J-M. Place, 1977.

————. "La Chasse d'Adonis," *L'Esprit créateur* 21, no. 4 (Winter 1981): 22–27.

Valéry, Paul. "Au sujet d'*Adonis.*" In *Oeuvres* de Paul Valéry, edited by Jean Hytier. 2 vols. Paris: Gallimard, Pléiade, 1957, 1: 474–95.

————. "Oraison funèbre d'une Fable," In ibid., 495–98.

Venesoen, Constant. "Un problème de paternité: Qui a écrit la *Dissertation sur Joconde?,*" *XVIIe Siècle,* 88 (1970): 31–48.

Vincent, Michael. " 'Fragmented Lovers' Discourse: Textuality and Sexuality in La Fontaine's *Les Deux Pigeons,*" *PFSCL* 9, no. 17 (1982): 675–90.

————. "Naming Names in La Fontaine's *Le Chat, la belette et le petit lapin,*" *Romanic Review* 73, no. 3 (May 1982): 292–301.

————. "Voice and Text: Representations of Reading in La Fontaine's *Psyché,*" *French Review* 57, no. 2 (Dec. 1983): 179–86.

————. "Transtextual Traps: *Le Rat et l'Huître,*" *PFSCL* 12, no. 22 (1985): 39–57.

Wadsworth, Philip. "La Fontaine As Student and Critic of Malherbe," *Symposium* 3 (1949): 130–39.

————. *Young La Fontaine. A Study of His Artistic Growth in His Early Poetry and First Fables.* Evanston, Ill.: Northwestern University Press, 1952. Outstanding and essential.

————. "La Fontaine and His Views on Marriage," *Rice University Studies,* 51, no. 3 (Summer 1965): 81–96.

————. "Ovid and La Fontaine," *Yale French Studies,* (May 1967): 151–55. Essays in Honor of Henri Peyre.

————. "The Art of Allegory in La Fontaine's *Fables,*" *French Review* 45, no. 6 (May 1972): 1125–35.

————. "Le Douzième Livre des *Fables,*" *CAIEF* 26 (mai 1974): 103–15.

————. "La Fontaine's Poems of Self-Appraisal," *PFSCL* 4/5 (Summer 1976): 57–74.

Youssef, Zobeidah. "Le Temps des amours dans l'onde irréversible: l'*A-donis* de La Fontaine," *Studi francesi* 65–66, (Maggio-dicembre 1978): 241–49.

————. *La Poésie de l'eau dans les Fables de La Fontaine.* Avant-propos de J-P. Collinet. *Biblio 17,* no. 3. Paris, Seattle, Tübingen, *PFSCL,* 1982. Bibliographie.

Zuber, Roger. "*Le Songe d'un habitant du Mogol:* étude littéraire," *Bulletin de la faculté des lettres de Strasbourg* 41 (1963): 361–70. Coauthor with Bernard Beugnot of *Boileau. Visages anciens, visages nouveaux,* 1665–1970.

6. Unpublished Dissertation
Logan, John L. "La Fontaine's *Psyche:* A Critical Study." Ph.D. dissertation, Yale University, 1975.

Index

DATE DUE

GAYLORD			PRINTED IN U.S.A.